the
Coffee Oracle

The Coffee Oracle © 2008 by Stacey Demarco

• *Published and distributed in Australia by:* Hay House Australia Pty. Ltd.: www.hayhouse.com.au • *Published and distributed in the United States by:* Hay House, Inc.: www.hayhouse.com • *Published and distributed in the United Kingdom by:* Hay House UK, Ltd.: www.hayhouse.co.uk • *Published and distributed in the Republic of South Africa by:* Hay House SA (Pty), Ltd.: www.hayhouse.co.za • *Distributed in Canada by: Raincoast:* www.raincoast.com • *Published in India by:* Hay House Publishers India: www.hayhouse.co.in

Cover and interior design by: Rhett Nacson
Symbols directory typesetting by: Bookhouse
Location photography by: Rapideye Photography. www.headshots.com.au
Location shots at: Sticky and Moo Cafe, Alexandria NSW Australia. www.stickyandmoo.com
Editorial team: Tamara Stanley, Verusha Singh, Maria Dominguez and Despina Rosales

ISBN 9781401918187

1st printing, September 2008
Printed in China by Imago

STACEY DEMARCO

the
Coffee Oracle

HAY HOUSE, INC.
Carlsbad, California • New York City
London • Sydney • Johannesburg
Vancouver • Hong Kong • New Delhi

'No one can understand
the Truth until he drinks
of coffee's frothy goodness.'

— Sheik Abd-al-Kadir
Algerian Sufi Scholar,
1808-1883

CONTENTS

Introduction part 1 . . . . . Worshipping at the Temple of Coffee 1
Introduction part 2 . . . . . What is an Oracle? 7

☕ SECTION 2
Chapter 1 . . . . The Rhythm and Ritual 19
Chapter 2 . . . . Reading the Coffee Oracle 27
Chapter 3 . . . . The Easy 5 Step Method 35
Chapter 4 . . . . The 28 Day Self-Discovery Plan 51

☕ THE SYMBOL DICTIONARY

A 67	J 157	S 239
B 77	K 163	T 261
C 97	L 169	U 277
D 113	M 179	V 281
E 119	N 191	W 287
F 125	O 197	X 299
G 135	P 203	Y 301
H 141	Q 227	Z 305
I 153	R 229	

☕ RESOURCES
Q and A 307
Animal Guides 311
The 28 Day Self–Discovery Plan Template 313

worshipping
at the
temple *of*
COFFEE

I remember as a little girl how much I loved going over to my auntie's house for a coffee afternoon. My auntie was married to a man of Greek birth and all her raven-haired Hellenic sisters-in-law would sweep grandly into her small, bright kitchen laden with big baking trays of warm sesame–sprinkled, plaited biscuits and honey-soaked pistachio pastries.

For a pigtailed, Bondi beach girl of five or six, this was unspeakably exotic, and I would watch wide-eyed as my mother, my auntie and all the Greek sisters would begin to unpack the 'tools' for our afternoon sojourn.

1

Unpacked first would be the special coffee cups – not the usual clunky mugs or tea cups we had at our house, but ones that were a completely different shape and almost translucent. They had no handles, were much narrower and were patterned in turquoise, rose and gold.

Then, out would come the gold foil bag of magic beans. I would always lean over and inhale the luminous brown, cowrie-shaped roasted beans, such was the hypnotic hold that smell had on me. Next, a wooden and steel coffee grinder would hit the table and lastly – unveiled with a flourish as a magician would a rabbit in a hat – the tall, brass engraved coffee pot.

I would watch as the women performed what seemed a complex choreographed dance, each movement linked by the promise of the black elixir that would eventually be poured, thick and glossy from the brass pot. The grinding, the measuring, and the boiling occurred time and time again until… a long pour was made into each cup, without a single drop spilled.

Then sugar was added. In fact, lashings of sugar were insisted upon. Then a whirling dervish of pastries, cakes and conversations began to fly across the steam-filled room.

As I was still a child, I wasn't permitted a taste of the rich, black potion that I so loved the aroma of. I could feast on all the sweet goodies I wanted, but the coffee was deemed "too strong for me". So I wouldn't feel too ostracised, my cup was filled with cola or dark grape juice so it would look like coffee.

I knew better of course and as I was, let's say politely, a persistent child, I certainly wasn't happy with this arrangement. After probably one too many complaints, like water wearing away stone, my mother was cajoled by the aunties into allowing me to drink hot milk with a teaspoon of the black coffee mixed in.

I was triumphant.

I loved 'my' coffee so much that my mother soon bought me my own coffee cup; a tiny china cup and saucer with a delicate floral pattern and a real gold rim. She told me that it was a coffee cup especially for little girls, (I now know it was an espresso cup!) and I was so proud to be able to join all the beautiful grown–up ladies in their special activity.

But the best was yet to come.

As the women around me drained their coffee, leaving scarlet lipstick marks on the rim, each in turn would go quiet for a small while, cradling the cup in both hands and allowing their eyes to hood. In one swift movement they would turn the cup upside down with a sharp click, let the dregs drain into the saucer, and then turn the cup a few times and then again, flip the cup the right way up.

All the energy would come back into their bodies like Christmas lights going on and all would gather around the cup in order to see what pictures the earthy grinds had made.

"Ooh, a visitor is coming…do you have that house of yours in order? Hahahah!"

"Ah! I see that you will travel soon. Maybe you can talk your husband into taking you to a tropical island rather than the caravan you slept in last year?"

"That new job of yours will be bringing in more money than you thought, hey?"

And sometimes more serious matters were raised and validated.

"Mmm…that decides it then. I will tell him what I think."

"Another child on the way…I hope you are ready!"

"I know I need to put myself first for a change. I feel so trapped but I know this is the way forward."

"Yes, change is coming. Good!"

Decades later, the memories of these afternoons are still vivid in my mind, yet two aspects have really stood out.

The first was the answer I got when I asked one of the aunties what they were doing when they peered into the coffee cups.

She pulled me onto her lap, her brown eyes meeting mine and said very seriously, "I am listening to my heart speak and to the sound of the God's voice. Both make pictures for us to look at."

And the second was how this revelation made me *feel*.

It made me feel powerful.

It made me feel secure.

And it made me feel very sure that she had told me the *truth*.

I realised that this was not a frightening or superstitious thing like the bogeyman or a monster. This wasn't some trick or some coincidence instead this was advice from something big and wise! It was a truth, just as real as the fact that my dog had brown fur and that I had to unfortunately go to school on Monday. And I was really glad about this because I felt that I was connected to something that made things simpler, not more complex. Something that made them – and me – feel like they knew what to do if we felt worried or sad and also feel closer to each other. Listening to my own heart or to God's made good sense, especially if it made me feel as calm and happy as I did in my auntie's kitchen.

As a grown woman I still feel the same way, although naturally I have a lot more going on than the six year old 'me'. Boy, it's a lot harder to hold on to that calm and happy feeling!

However, I have learnt that divination or Oracle reading in some form enables me to quickly connect with my own deep Self and with the Divine. By engaging an Oracle, I know I am actively co–creating with 'something bigger' and getting clear about the next steps forward. I can cut through the fog of confusion, leap-frog over fear or plan my next fiscal quarter by side–stepping my rational conscious mind and choosing to listen to something bigger and wiser.

By consulting a really convenient Oracle, such as the one in your coffee cup, not only can you stay open and connected to your own intuition and creative powers more often but to the Divine as well…a very potent combination in this increasingly disconnected world.

Coffee connects us, stimulates and opens our minds and hearts for conversation of the inner and outer kind. As a busy businesswoman, author, and Witch (not necessarily in that order!), I have learned to weave a Coffee Oracle into my daily life. The form this normally takes – a visit to a café for a takeaway – is a decidedly modern yet ritualistic activity for me and has enriched my life both spiritually and materially. I am certain that it will do the same for you.

For those who don't feel they have, or wish to have, a 'spiritual' bent, coffee can still be seen at the very least, as a reviver, a pick–me–up, an activity that gives a small breather in an ordinarily frantic day, or as a conversation starter. I invite you to put any preconceived ideas to the side and simply enter into consulting the Coffee Oracle with a sense of fun and discovery. Just like reading shapes in clouds or seeing pictures in the open fire, allow your imagination to run wild, relax and see what comes of it. You may be mightily surprised!

What I love about reading coffee is that you don't have to have an intense knowledge about coffee or any fancy equipment. You can consult the Oracle on the train on your way to work, at your office desk, in a busy cafe, or even tucked up in bed. Gone are the days where you have to know, as my aunties did, how to brew traditional, thick, Middle Eastern-style coffee to get a reliable reading. You don't even have to have a special cup, although funnily enough I'm still drinking out of small cups (espresso is my Oracle of choice!). Now, it can be as simple as popping in and paying a quick visit to your friendly neighbourhood barista.

I consider myself a very rational person and I normally take quite a bit of convincing to feel sure something doesn't just work for me but works consistently for others too. As such, I collect case studies and record methods to prove and ensure success. This book is the result of many years of practical experience, research, case studies and results that stretch well beyond what most people would term coincidence.

I would love you to treat my book as a coffee companion, a small, friendly guide that can easily be carried solo into your local café – or noisily shared with friends. See it as an instruction book that suggests rituals and paths to follow towards the better hearing of one's own heart's desires and perhaps a decoder of some of the harder puzzles that get in our way.

Above all, I hope that you never see your humble cup of coffee in quite the same way again.

So come join me for coffee, won't you?

part two

what is an
ORACLE?

lthough we are born with everything we need to realise our purpose, there are times in life when we feel less than sure of ourselves. Maybe we have an important decision to make and it is one that seems to have far–reaching consequences if we 'get it wrong'. Perhaps we keep making the same mistakes over and over, and somewhere lurks a pattern that no longer serves us but we haven't got the eyes to track it or the strength to break it.

Alternatively, the pressure of life is wearing us down and we don't feel as powerful as we should, and reaching within ourselves for a reliable answer to a problem seems impossible.

Haven't we all at some time felt the need for a sound piece of advice or craved the ear of a wise, learned friend?

Looking back to some of your harder decisions with perfect hindsight, wouldn't you have felt less pressured and more confident if you could have had a satisfying conversation with someone who you knew would give you wise counsel?

Our ancient ancestors, when faced with situations such as these, would have felt happy to release the pressure upon themselves and consult an Oracle to assist them. Whether you were a king or conqueror, a maid or farmer, an Oracle would be within your reach.

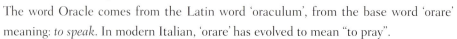

but what exactly is an oracle?

The word Oracle comes from the Latin word 'oraculum', from the base word 'orare' meaning: *to speak*. In modern Italian, 'orare' has evolved to mean "to pray".

Oracles are the means in which energies, normally the Divine and our own deep Selves, come forward together to 'speak' and give actionable insights.

Please note the terminology I use: ACTIONABLE INSIGHTS. These are not unachievable ideas or freewheeling airy–fairy advice that doesn't have a purpose. These are insights directly relevant to our life or the problem at hand and they *are actionable right now*.

Oracles enable us to refocus our energies, and encourage us to exercise our intuition and imagination. They validate our own considerable power and make decision–making easier and faster. They can offer a new solution or simply a second opinion. They give us back the peace of mind and confidence in our own personal sovereignty to be able to make the changes and transformations that we seek. In some ways, they may even be the answer to our 'prayers'.

An Oracle can be the midwife to the birth of a new you.

what are some examples of oracles?

In ancient times, when we were much closer to the cycles of the Earth and the natural world around us, messages from the Gods could be seen and interpreted as just a part of life. Our ancestors would look for signals and symbols in the colour of the sky, in the song of a bird, or in the random way raindrops would fall upon a stone. An unexpected animal visitor could be a portent for a feast or famine – or the whispering of the wind a message straight from a Goddess's lips.

In ancient Britain, women would shake herbs over a white cloth and allow the seeds to drop. The patterns that would fall indicated the future for their family or gave the timing for their next child. The New Zealand Maori would throw three stones into the lake and the way the stones would enter the water would indicate important information about the caster's past, present or future.

The Ethiopians would toss coffee beans on a brass plate and watch how many fell off the plate and how many remained. The numbers indicated various future scenarios such as whether this year's harvest would be successful or if it was time to sell off their cattle for the best profit. Some Native American and indigenous Australian tribes paid special attention to dreams and created highly complex rituals and art around the predictions and symbology of the dreamtime.

Some cultures, such as the Mayan and Egyptian, would make animal blood sacrifices and 'read' the entrails or organs of the creature for signs that would indicate the path to take. These practices still remain honoured in many communities today.

During a recent trip to the remote Indonesian Island of Sumba, I watched as the Ratu (the animist priests) sacrificed a chicken and examined the liver closely for irregularities and dark spots which would indicate a bad omen before a seasonal fertility festival. The priests concluded that during the 'Pasola', (a wild spear–throwing battle conducted on horseback), there would be blood spilled that year but no one would be killed. The community was happy to hear this, and sure enough, spears did pierce skin with some small amounts of blood spilled upon the soil (including mine!) but no one was mortally wounded. There are written records of the priests interpretations over the years and they have rarely been wrong.

I personally have experienced a powerful Oracle on the way to a job interview. I had decided to pursue a position for all the wrong reasons. I knew I had an issue ethically with this company, and knew that the fixed contract would limit my freedom in some way, but the role paid incredibly well. The salary was almost double what I was earning at the time! I was one of only two people invited to an interview for the position so I thought this made me 'special'. Although every intuitive alarm bell was ringing in my ears, I still decided to go.

As I drove along, I accidentally went the wrong way and passed through a beautiful tree–lined street. The sun was shining and it dappled through the branches. Native birds flitted across the paths. I was actually thinking how beautiful it was compared to the busy highway I was just on.

Although I was traveling well under the speed limit, I suddenly ran over one of the birds. I was horrified. I had never killed anything before. I knew immediately that this was a very bad omen. What came to me incredibly clearly as I stood over that poor bird's body, was that my freedom was in jeopardy and I should never have come.

But it was ten minutes to my appointment and I thought it would be unprofessional to cancel. I placed the bird on the grass and managed to arrive on time. I met the CEO of this major multinational company and it was the single most horrific interview I have ever had. Not only did he confirm my ethical concerns about them, he was quite misogynistic and egotistical on top of it all! If only I had listened to my own intuition and the powerful Oracle that I was sent.

Sometimes, the Oracles have indeed been living creatures, often people. In these cases the Universe speaks through a person and the message may be directly interpreted by the receiver or through a priest or priestess. The most famous Oracle in this form was that of Delphi in Ancient Greece.

Dedicated to the god Apollo, we know that the Delphic Oracle was consulted by some of the most famous generals and conquerors of the ancient world including Caesar, Alexander the Great and Croesus of Lydia such was its power and political influence for over a thousand years.

The Delphic Oracle itself, or should I say 'herself', was always a woman. She sat upon a tri–legged stool upon a rock and breathed in the vapors that rose mysteriously from a fissure near a sacred spring. This beautiful, yet somewhat harsh place, was considered by the Greeks as the spot where Apollo himself chose to speak and that it was the 'omphalos' (centre) of the known universe.

The Delphic Oracle would answer questions posed to her by supplicants and normally the answers would be in riddles, verses or in an unknown language. These then would normally be interpreted by the priest or priestess serving the Oracle. However, the final decision on true interpretation was always left to the questioner. They needed to add their own intuition to the mix so that there was no interference with free will.

Another famous Oracle, who was said to have received his gift from Apollo himself was a man named Calchas. Calchas was the seer who accompanied the Achaeans to the Trojan War and offered warning and counsel. His story and his words have survived today through written and oral Greek stories.

Of course the more modern aspects of consulting an Oracle no longer involve delving into any kind of blood sacrifice, and often without the intermediary of a dedicated priest or priestess.

Take a walk into any New Age shop and you are surrounded by potential Oracles. Runes are a kind of Oracle, as are the Tarot, and the I–Ching. All can be consulted by anyone with some time and training. But now, you can consult an Oracle through drinking a cup of coffee from your local cafe! Forget months of training, you can start with your morning cuppa!

oracles have a common anatomy.

There are some common attributes of Oracles and they are:

1. There must be a random aspect so there is no way of controlling or influencing the outcome.
2. There is normally a symbolic language that needs to be understood and interpreted to give a structure to the consultation.
3. There is an equal need for imagination/intuition.
4. There is a call to action but no interference with free will.

So how do these attributes apply to our Coffee Oracle?

1. There is a random aspect

Every cup of coffee is different. Even if it's created by the same barista, with the same brand of coffee beans in the same machine, it will be different than the coffee he/she made for you yesterday or even a half an hour before.

The way you feel, the energies around the barista, how many beans fall into the grinder, how hot the water is, how creamy the foam is and how many grinds finally settle at the bottom of the cup are all steps in the process that have literally millions of variables. There is no way, unless you manually interfere with the patterns made in the cup, that you can alter what appears there.

2. There is normally a symbolic language that needs to be understood and interpreted to give structure and meaning to the consultation.

In some cultures, a high-ranking priest or holy woman was the only one allowed to interpret the Oracle and the only ones who knew the rules for decoding the symbology. In others, years of training were required to be even allowed to witness an Oracle–based ritual, let alone be at the centre of one.

Happily, you now have it a little easier than that! Simply turn to the Oracle Symbol Dictionary which will give some structure to the patterns and symbols you may be seeing.

I have gathered traditional and ancient interpretations of the symbols plus many of the insights I have gathered through years of real–life case studies. I would also encourage you to add symbols of your own as they appear and you 'prove' them as time goes on. I would also recommend that you relate your experiences with other like-minds. This way, our modern interpretations grow and evolve to suit the kind of life we live now.

☕ 3. There is also an equal need for imagination/intuition.

In this book I will be sharing with you a foolproof step-by-step guide on how to read your own Coffee Oracle.

You will discover that there are a few small but very important actions you need to take prior to sipping that cup and then prior to turning the cup back over to read it.

One of those actions is to take the time to connect with your inner Self, and with what the Self needs and desires at that moment. Clearing the mind of everyday matters and focusing on the question at hand facilitates precise and powerful Oracle work. I will show you a few simple methods to do this successfully anywhere, anytime.

Getting in touch with our deeper Selves frees up our unconscious and allows it expression without the restriction of the rational mind. These expressions speak a vastly different 'language' than the rational mind. The deeper Self, or unconscious, speaks in (and understands) feelings, aromas, colours, and symbols…perfect coffee language!

Combine our own intuition with the interpretation of the more 'rational' symbols and you have a highly accurate and wise 'voice' to listen to: a true Oracle.

☕ 4. There is a call to action but no interference with free will.
When you combine the opening of the mind and inner Self, allowing intuition 'to speak' through the language of the symbols, there is more often than not, a clear path to tread. However, no matter how obvious the message, it is very important to know that the decision to heed that message is yours and yours alone.

This Oracle message certainly may well be wise counsel from the highest places … yet you are free to choose what steps to take next and when. This is where the Universe demonstrates co-creation. You choose. No power is making you do anything.

A warning though…do not let fear alone hold you back.

let me give you an example.
Sharon is a 35-year-old sales professional who felt stymied in her current role mainly because of an overbearing manager, and began to look for something else. Sharon applied for a number of jobs and even though she was qualified she wasn't picking up any of the roles. She began to consult the Coffee Oracle in her morning espresso over three days.

What she found was that there was indeed a role coming very soon and it had a number of travel symbols connected to it (aeroplane, water, feet). She also noted that a symbol that looked like a monster to her appeared on the edge of her cup (meaning fear or unfounded fears).

The next day, a recruitment consultant rang her with a great sales opportunity that would involve travel. In fact, it was in the travel industry. Sharon applied and was soon offered the job on Friday. She told the consultant that she would give her an answer on the Monday so she could consider her options. It all seemed very quick and easy… which worried Sharon. What seemed like a great job now seemed too big, too hard and she was likely to fail. Even her boyfriend commented that it was a big step up.

She began to think it would be better to stay where she was. By the Sunday night she had convinced herself not to take the position and was prepared to turn down the job the next day.

Monday morning came. She had decided to call the consultant and say no to the role. However, before she made the call she decided to go to her favourite café and grab herself an espresso and see what the Oracle said.

"It's the least I can do," she said to herself.

In her cup appeared a phoenix, a symbol of success over fear and adversity. She realised, right there in that busy coffee shop, that it was only her fear standing in the way of a fantastic opportunity.

She took the role, and within a year she was promoted even further and almost doubled her income.

If your intuition is signaling strongly that a new option is the right one, move confidently as your fear may just be the rational mind taking control again.

As we are consulting coffee, it is in the participation department that we have a definite advantage! Allow the stimulating and reviving qualities of coffee to make it easy to motivate yourself gently into action, no matter what form that may take.

Do as Sharon now says:

"Let that coffee kick you where you need it to get you moving!"

something
new is
brewing

the modern
art of the
coffee oracle

the RHYTHM and RITUAL

I am sitting in my favourite local café. I have my laptop out on the small laminated table and I'm sitting close to the wide open doors, quietly watching.

No one notices me now, but earlier I've been greeted intimately by the barista nodding and saying, "The usual?"

It's early, it's a work day, and there is a steady stream of people walking in and ordering their coffee.

¡A skim cap, thanks.¡

¡Weak latte.¡

¡Two espressos to go.¡

¡Short mac, ta mate.¡

It is almost poetry. Or haiku.

Some stand and drink it European-style at the bar and door. Others grab their paper cups and run onwards to big days just glimpsed. Some sit, sprawled over a newspaper, coffee warming one hand, pages turning with the other, their eyes shining and scanning.

They are all here, worshipping at the Temple of Coffee.

I listen closely.

Bang bang bang

Grrrrrrrrrrrrrrrr

Click click click

Ting ting ting

Crunch

Shhhhhhhh!

Dribbledribbledribbledribble

Again:

Bang bang bang (emptying the old coffee out of the coffee handle)

Grrrrrrrrrrrrrrrr (the coffee beans are ground)

Click click click (clicking the grinder handle to drop the ground coffee into the metal coffee handle)

Ting ting ting (the pestle is hit on the side of the handle to settle the coffee)

Crunch (the pestle presses the coffee tight into the handle)

Shhhhhhhh! (steam and magic)

Dribbledribbledribbledribble (the coffee flows)

It's a definite rhythm.

It is ancient like African drums and modern like electronic dance music. Strangely, I'm surprised at how melodious it is. I wonder if anyone else has noticed and I realise that of course we all do, but quite unconsciously. This is always part of the experience for us; it is part of what draws us to coffee... the sound, the repetition, the ritual.

I have also found that most great baristas have a very set rhythm and their own small rituals. The barista here has a certain way of spinning the pestle prior to crunching the coffee down flat. I'm thinking it's a bit like one of those juggling bar tenders tossing up a shaker like a juggling pin.

I ask him as I leave, "I love the way you spin the pestle. Why do you do it?"

He looks embarrassed, surprised and pleased at the same time.

"Do I?" he says, his fair cheeks reddening. "I don't think about it. It's just the way I make the coffee. It's a habit I guess, a bit of a ritual."

It just happens that this ritual is the perfect way to midwife the Oracle process.

the role of the barista

Each barista handles every single coffee differently. Each barista handles each machine differently. There is randomness and a purpose to it and as you have learnt, we know we need this for any true Oracle system.

This rhythm and process is almost like a trance in great baristas. Their focus and concentration is immense. They have to combine a physical and a mental act so there is little, if any, opportunity to think about anything else. Just like sportspeople who, to use a modern term, get into the 'zone', a barista who is in the flow is not thinking about anything else and so opens themselves to their unconscious far more readily. Show me a barista who isn't in the zone even for a short while and I'll show you a bad coffee!

This zone, flow or trance state is very useful for the delivery of the Oracle in that it provides a purity and connection to a greater Universal power.

I have watched priests and priestesses, holy men and women of all traditions and some very talented psychics, and there is a common behaviour in the way they work. There is always a level of allowance or 'letting go and letting the Universe speak'. There is always an element of trance or flow.

As a Witch and practitioner of some of the ancient arts, I experience this often and it's a hard state to explain other than saying everything is easy and the answers virtually leap out at you. This is not necessarily a passive feeling but one of quiet vitality, and often there is little memory of what you did and said in that state.

I have read Oracles for people, performed complex rituals and even written large sections of my books and couldn't remember the details of what happened, just that it felt good and was 'right'.

You don't have to be a Witch though, to know what this feels like. Most of us have experienced how powerful this 'trance' is simply by driving a car.

If you have been driving a car for a number of years, all the actions become quite unconscious in that you don't actually think about most of the individual mechanical processes like turning the key, steering, putting on indicators, etc. You just do it. Most of us decide where we are going, start our car and really can't remember how we got there! This is a great example of the separation of the conscious and unconscious minds at work, and how flow works on a very basic level.

So if we think about the role of the barista in our Coffee Oracle, he or she could be likened to the traditional priest or priestess creating the circumstances for the Oracle. The main difference with the Coffee Oracle is however, and this is a very modern difference, that it will be you who will be deciphering or reading the Oracle, not them. It will be you who will empower yourself by being able to gain actionable insights from the omens in your cup. It will be you who will take action to get what you most desire.

But what about the personal energy of the barista? Doesn't this have some impact?

Baristas are often super busy and have a reputation of being slightly on the cranky side, a bit like chefs. Often I am asked, can a cranky barista change the energy or outcome of my coffee? The short answer is yes – but with a big BUT.

If the barista's crankiness interrupted their flow and therefore their ability to allow a totally random and rhythmic force into their body and mind, then yes. What's more, you'll probably get a nasty coffee to boot. However, by far, it is *your* energy, *your* intuition and *your* interpretation that will dominate the outcome of your Coffee Oracle.

My recommendation is to know your barista or choose one based on feeling your own reaction to them. Do you feel positive emotions or neutral emotions when seeing or interacting with them? If so, go for it. If you feel like someone isn't right for you, they probably are not.

styles of coffee:

I am often asked whether the style of coffee people prefer can change the outcome of the Oracle.

Whether you love a frothy cappuccino, a powerful espresso or a milky latte, it makes absolutely no difference to the nature of the reading. What it will do though is change somewhat the process of how you read the symbols, (for example, you would read the froth residue in a cappuccino but the crema in an espresso), but more of that later.

What I have discovered though are some similarities between the attributes of people who do prefer certain styles of coffee. You may find the following information on the most common styles useful and fun, particularly as it may give you further insight into someone's personality or preferences if you do happen to be reading with or for them.

STYLE	PERSONAL ATTRIBUTES
Cappuccino >	Luxury-loving, pleasure-seeking, family orientated
Latte >	Likes creature comforts, playful, friendly
Macchiato >	Adventurous, creative, ideas person, curious
Espresso (short black) >	No-nonsense, passionate, creative, inventive, individualistic, complex
Long Black >	Good attention to detail, insightful
Flat White >	Calm, thoughtful, slightly introverted, inner life is important
Affagato >	Daring, artistic, fun-loving, can seem tough but actually very softhearted
Mocha >	Good listeners, able to see both sides of a story, tolerant
Piccolo >	Enjoys attention, likes to make big statements, positive, social
Asking for a STRONG version >	Appreciates quality over quantity, driven, focused

the kind of coffee:

Although it is an extremely romantic and a lovely process, most of us do not have the time or expertise to brew up a thick, multiple-boiled Middle Eastern style coffee. This is the kind of coffee that people often expect to be the only one to use in Oracle reading. Of course, that's not true as you are quickly discovering.

The kind of coffee used does not matter to the end result of the reading – with one big exception. Do not use instant coffee as it leaves little real residue and is so chemically treated it really isn't coffee any more!

The best results are from barista-made coffee or from a good home or office coffee machine or a European stove-top pot.

I would also ask that you note that filtered coffee, made from processed coffee (similar to instant) is also not suitable. The basic 'rule of thumb' is that if it forms a crema, which is the gold-coloured silky film on the top after it is brewed, the coffee is perfect for Oracle purposes.

CHAPTER TWO

reading the coffee oracle

i have been reading coffee as an Oracle for many years and just like the barista in my local café, I rarely thought about how I did it either. It has become second nature to me now. But when I began writing this book, I knew one of the key parts of my sharing the knowledge with you would be communicating and teaching you how to read coffee accurately yourself, and that I would have to break down into detail what it was that I did *exactly*.

So I decided to do this two ways to be sure to gain an objective view of the process. Write down what I thought I did, and also get friends to watch what I did. I added this together. And now, when I pass my techniques through to you, you can be certain that this is a tried and tested method and the process is described in such a way that you can learn and practice the same way easily.

I have great news for you. The process is very simple!

In fact, just like making a coffee, there is a set of five simple steps to follow. Do what I suggest and you will be reading straight away.

I also have interesting news for you. The process will be very much your own!

Like coffee making, the magic, the quality, and the difference in a great insightful reading, is in your own little magic and rituals. I have often marveled how two baristas on the one machine, doing what looks like the same things, can produce two very different kinds of coffee. Just like them, you will be interpreting the symbology *your* way and with *your* deep intuition. Exciting!

A quick anatomy lesson first and we will be on our way...

anatomy of the coffee cup:

As with any Oracle, there are a set of guidelines to reading accurately, so allow me to start with the easiest – that of the coffee cup itself.

With the Coffee Oracle there are two interconnecting areas: the cup and the symbols themselves.

The coffee cup, whether it is plastic, paper or the finest china, has certain physical areas that lend themselves to certain insights. These insights may allude to timing, positivity/negativity, different people, or even spiritual levels.

We layer these insights over the symbols.

On the next page is a picture of an average coffee cup with these areas clearly marked out for you.

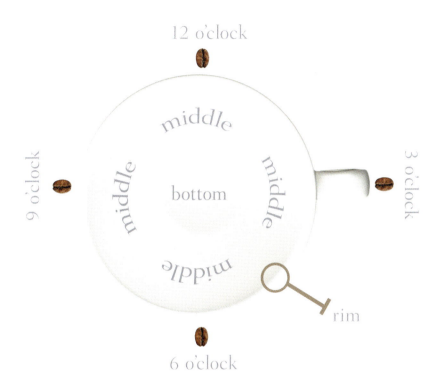

let's look at each section in some detail.

☕ *the rim:*

The rim is the area closest to where you drink. This is the area of the cup that indicates timing-wise things that will happen right now or in the short term. This is an extremely positive section of the cup and indicates forward movement. It also represents the spiritual aspect of the message.

🍵 *the middle:*

This is the rest of the main area of the cup. The middle encompasses all areas except for the near bottom and bottom of the cup. Here, things that will occur will do so in the midterm, and the closer to the bottom the further the timing is in the future. It also represents the cerebral aspect of the message.

🍵 *the bottom:*

This is the base of the inside of the cup and just before the edge. This is an area of the cup where negative issues are displayed. Timing-wise, it alludes to a long way into the future or not at all. It also represents the physical aspect.

next, we can look at the quarters of the cup:

In tasseography, (tea reading) practitioners place a lot of emphasis on the placement of the handle in order for them to navigate their way around specific sections of the cup. Unlike the old fashioned teacups, almost three quarters of the coffee cups I drink from have no handle! Yep, try hanging on to one of those tiny paper handles in the car... a sure recipe for paying a visit to your friendly drycleaner or doctor!

So when you decide to read your coffee cup, just mentally imagine a clock face over the top of your cup. You will then decide where 12 o'clock is, then accordingly 3 o'clock, 6 o'clock and finally 9 o'clock. The 6 o'clock position should be the position closest to your mouth when you drink.

what each area means:

☕ **12 o'clock:** Spiritual, higher support, far distance

☕ **3 o'clock:** Physical, family, support, the future

☕ **6 o'clock:** Represents the Enquirer (the person who is asking the Oracle), close distance, closest people to you, purpose

☕ **9 o'clock:** Obstacles, opposites, adversaries, the past

the symbols:

So once we have familiarised ourselves with the anatomy of our cup, we can then overlay the real stars of the show: our Oracle Symbols.

You may see one or more of these symbols in your cup, and they could be placed anywhere within that cup…and occasionally they may even leap out off the rim!

In the Section three of this book, you will find a **Symbol Dictionary**. Here, listed in alphabetical order conveniently for you, are hundreds of symbols, each with their key messages, Oraclic message and some additional insights which may help clarify your reading further.

The symbols I have chosen are the ones that seem to crop up most commonly for me and for others who read the Coffee Oracle. Some are ancient symbols, such as an ankh, unicorn or a bow and arrow, that still resonate with our modern lives. Some symbols are modern however, like a computer or mobile phone.

The meaning of each symbol is often a mixture of ancient wisdom, the nature of the physical object, or the observance of the results of that symbol. Let me give you an example:

an apple appears in your cup:

The ancient symbology of apples tells us that they signify temptation, wisdom and new beginnings. The Adam and Eve story is an example of this symbolism amongst others.

The nature of the object tells us that they are healthy, beneficial and 'positive'.

I have observed as a result over many readings that an apple may end up meaning a foray into technology, (reflecting that popular brand of computer). Two readings in a row showed an apple and both people ended up working for that company!

So, as a reflection of these three areas, the key messages for the symbol of an apple that I have listed are: teaching and knowledge, new beginnings, a temptation, an opportunity, good health, IT or computers.

Knowing how symbols are defined may also assist you greatly if there is a symbol in your cup that is not listed in the dictionary. Take those three areas and see if you can decipher the symbol you can see yourself. If you are really stuck, I welcome your questions and comments via email at Stacey@themodernwitch.com and we will work out the puzzle together!

combining the cup and the symbols:

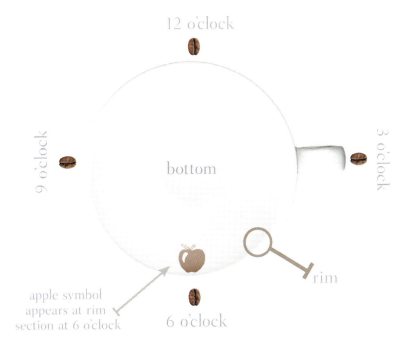

Let's imagine that you have indeed spotted an apple, and it is sitting in at the rim of your cup in the 6 o'clock position.

From overlaying our anatomy, this can be construed as 'something' is going to happen very quickly or immediately definitely with or to YOU. This 'something' will have everything to do with the key messages of learning, wisdom, new beginnings, etc.

The big question though remains: What specifically is this 'something'?

What that 'something' is, depends greatly on the question that you have focused on asking prior to looking in the cup or other symbols in the cup. This question now brings me to the exciting part, which is showing you exactly how a reading works, exactly how to challenge and develop your intuitive Self and exactly how to discover that 'something'.

Curious? Great. Let's go!

the easy **5** step method

There are five steps to consulting the Coffee Oracle. These are:

- ☕ **FOCUS:** Your question or enquiry
- ☕ **RAISING POWER:** Buying the coffee, drinking the coffee
- ☕ **RELEASE:** Question, turning and releasing
- ☕ **INTERPRETATION:** Reading and deciphering
- ☕ **PARTICIPATION:** Taking action

1. focus:

In my consultative practice, people of all ages, nationalities, sexes and occupations are attracted to seeking some assistance to relieve them of some mental or physical pain, or to help them fulfill their desires.

focus

raising power

release

interpretation

participation

Trouble is, during the session when I begin to really dig, asking them to focus on their intention, they don't actually know what it is that they really want!

There is a myriad of reasons for this, but the two most common reasons are quite interesting.

The first reason is that people do not concentrate on themselves enough.

Some of my clients could tell you clearly what they think their partner wants or what their children desire, but not themselves. They just haven't thought about satisfying their own needs for some time. Make no mistake, knowing what you want and satisfying those desires is not a selfish act. It's an abundantly healthy act.

Without satisfying what you want or even asking the question, toxic emotions such as resentment, jealousy, restlessness and anger can easily build up, causing pain to yourself and others.

The second reason that people do not know what they want is that their conscious mind protects them from failure by not allowing them to do what it is that they really want.

This is normally characterised by someone who repeatedly 'almost' becomes successful or has a pattern of starting things and not completing them. These people can choke or get 'confused' when they get close to their purpose or goal. I call this getting a '*touch of the fuzzies*'.

why would our conscious rational mind do this to harm us?

Well, in truth, our rational mind would never purposefully harm us or make us unhappy. It only ever does things with a positive intent.

A positive intent? What could be the positive intent of making me fail time and time again, you ask?

The positive intent is one of protection. You can't get hurt if you don't try. You can't get hurt if you don't take risks and stay where you are, at the level you are, unchanged. If you stay safe and unchanged, you will not be disappointed or get hurt.

Of course this is a false assumption. You do get hurt and you do suffer accordingly. We suffer from the pain of non-achievement and we regret that we didn't do what we dreamed of. We suffer the agony of making the same mistake over and over. We do become beaten down by our rational mind being the loving jailer to our dreams. And all along, our unconscious mind, the part of us that knows our purpose and communicates our true intentions, gets trapped and buried, destined only to peak out at the odd times when the jailer isn't looking.

But there is hope.

By using an Oracle, such as the Coffee Oracle, we begin to bypass the rational conscious mind and we allow our unconscious mind to run free. By using symbols, we exercise our intuition, which is the voice of the unconscious. Whilst our rational mind is literally having a coffee, our unconscious mind is exchanging ideas with the Oracle and redirecting and reprogramming the conscious mind to be more 'on purpose'.

So, the first step in our Coffee Oracle consultation is that of FOCUS.

Decide to a have a coffee and decide to consult the Oracle within that coffee. This intent signals to the Universe that you wish to converse with it and the unconscious begins to prepare itself.

Then, decide what question you want answers to. Keep this question (or questions) clear and simple.

what kind of questions can I ask?

You can ask the Coffee Oracle all manner of questions from any area of your life or beyond!

You might consider querying the Oracle about areas of your life such as relationships, career, abundance, health and spirituality.

The Oracle is very useful for testing the validity of ideas, generating creative direction and helping with sound decision-making should you find yourself at a crossroads.

You may also ask the Oracle about issues of healing past trauma or how to handle tricky situations. The Oracle is also wonderful for getting a straight answer about someone or something that you are intuitively doubtful of or to clarify motives.

There is power in both broad and specific questions.

By asking deceptively simple broadly phased questions such as: "What do I want?" or "What do I need to know?", we affectively allow the unconscious mind free reign and tune into some high-level guidance.

If we have more specific questions such as: "Will I land this job I applied for?" or "I wish to attract a partner. Will this happen?", the Oracle can also answer these too, and give us additional information.

Once you have the intended enquiry in your mind or written down, you are ready for Step 2.

2. raising power

Now it's time to buy your coffee.

As you order your coffee, keep your enquiry in your mind. As you wait for the coffee, begin to focus on the rhythmic movements of the barista, the hiss of the steam and the aroma of coffee in the café. In fact, open up all your senses. This is an important step in opening all the psychic channels. We are 'sense-uous' beings and by opening our five senses as fully as we can, this triggers our sixth-our intuition.

When you receive the coffee, be seated if you are standing. Then, holding the cup in both hands, state your question out loud. Yes, that's right, out loud. By stating our intention out loud it further imbeds it into our unconscious mind and states it clearly to the Universe. Fear not, my good Enquirer; no one is going to think that you're crazy! You only need to whisper your question, no one need hear.

If you are with a friend who is going to consult the Coffee Oracle too though, feel free to share your intended question.

Then, breathe deeply and relax as much as you can. Take your time here. Soften your eyes, allow your body to relax, and take your first look at the cup and the patterns on top. Make a mental note of, or jot down on paper, anything that strikes you about the appearance of the coffee crema or foam. Then begin to sip your delicious cup of coffee.

Allow your mind to wander and then wander back to the question at hand. Don't try to control things too much. Just enjoy your coffee and the feeling of goodwill that it gives you.

If you are having a coffee with a group and you wish to read your cup but feel that holding a conversation is just as important, you can certainly do both! Just ensure that you allow your mind to wander back to your intended enquiry at regular intervals. It is important to feel good during this process to get a result, so do enjoy yourself and the coffee.

3. release

- ✔ When you have finished your coffee, it is now time to release the Oracle.
- ✔ Breathe deeply and state your question out loud again.
- ✔ Then, take your clean saucer (or secure lid) and place it upturned on the top of your cup.

✔ Holding the two tightly together, invert them both so now the saucer is on the bottom, and the cup is sitting upside down on the saucer. Place them on a hard surface.

✓ Turn the cup clockwise three times with your left hand.

- ✔ Then quickly turn it right side up.
- ✔ You should be able to see inside clearly. Do not swish or move the coffee too roughly!

- ✔ You have now released the Coffee Oracle and the symbols will begin to appear in your cup.

4. interpretation

Directly in front of you now sits the answer to your question.

There will be one or more symbols in a variety of areas in your cup. Depending upon the kind of coffee you are drinking, the symbols may be formed out of milk foam, chocolate, coffee grinds or crema.

It is very important that you do not just look for coffee grinds. Remember, we are not doing the old-fashioned readings here! You must regard and read the whole cup.

Often, with milky coffees such a lattes or flat whites there will be few grinds or dark coffee stains to spot, so you must look very closely at the milk or foam trail for your symbols.

If you cannot see any symbols, don't panic. They will appear eventually.

Quickly determine the 12 o'clock position and then the other anatomy should naturally follow.

Then begin to search for symbols. If possible, memorise or write down your first impressions or any symbols that appear early on. These symbols may change within minutes, so do work quickly. Then allow the coffee to transform, merge and solidify into magical, readable symbols.

There is no right or wrong here and first impressions count for a lot. If you "think" you see a "person" and it looks like your Uncle Fred, it's Uncle Fred. If you "think" a stain of milk resembles a "rabbit", that's what it is. If you spot a strangely shaped blob of foam that to you looks like a castle, even though no one else at your table sees it that way, I assure you, a castle has indeed built itself in your cup.

Editing the process by debating and changing what you see constantly is simply letting your rational conscious mind have full control again…and that's not what we want, is it? So decide what symbols are present, and where, and get on with deciphering them.

Once you have your symbols you can now piece together the puzzle.

Consult the Symbol Dictionary to elicit the meanings. What is imperative is that you weave these meanings and messages through your question. Depending on what you were asking, the symbols may mean different things, and so, here is where your skill at allowing your intuition to build the bridges comes in.

let me give you a real life example:

Julieann is a 30-year-old legal secretary who felt restless in her current role. It was a solid job that paid well, but did not challenge her.

Julieann's enquiry to the Oracle was: "Should I move on from my current job?"

the coffee oracle produced the following symbols:

- A kite – key messages: aspirations and ambition, positioned near the rim
- A kangaroo – key messages: moving forward leaps and bounds, positioned in the middle
- A paintbrush – key messages: variety and change, positioned at 6 o'clock

So, if we weave Julieann's enquiry through the symbols, what answer do you think she received?

julieann writes:

"I took the kite to mean that right now, I had big ambitions and dreams to do better. My job was safe, but not really the kind of position that I know will take me to where I want to go. The kangaroo showed me that I would be leaping forward and really moving in the

mid-term and I was really happy about that. But it was the paintbrush that really answered my question directly. It was an omen of change. A new coat of paint…a fresh start. The reading gave me the confidence to begin looking for a new job."

Less than three weeks after completing the reading, deciding to apply for new roles, and sending off her resume, Julieann was headhunted by another firm she had not even applied to. She accepted a role with great prospects and more salary.

At time of writing, it has been six months since beginning her new job and she comments, "You know without consulting the Oracle I probably wouldn't have had the impetus to move on from my old job. I am now moving ahead in leaps and bounds just as that lovely kangaroo suggested."

Julieann was able to weave the key messages of the three quite different symbols into a meaning that felt 'right' for her. You too will be able to do this very easily and it only gets more enjoyable as time passes! Your confidence in your own intuitive power will build steadily and the Oracle process will speed up considerably. Soon, consulting your daily cuppa will be second nature.

5. participation

As you can see from Julieann's story, what she did after the reading was integral to her success. Her actions made the difference.

Immediately after the reading, she made the decision to change jobs. She then went back into her everyday world and began to take actions to begin that process. As it happened, the Universe co-created a great job with her – one that she least expected – and now she has what she desired.

In my experience, too many people consult the Oracle and then do nothing about it afterwards. The whole process of the Coffee Oracle is such an enjoyable one that bothering about the pesky 'real world' later isn't that attractive.

Often, people get very good at discovering what their unconscious and the Universe has in store for them. Their intuitive abilities build. Their psychic channels open. They can even do incredibly accurate readings for others and facilitate their clients' successes. Yet, they do not follow through with their own participation. They end up not getting what they have had foretold or what they want!

The final step in the Coffee Oracle consultation is **participation**. I may have labelled it number five but it certainly is not the least important.

I cannot urge you strongly enough to put into action what you have discovered. You must ACT on the messages the Oracle reveals to you. Why consult an Oracle of any type if you do not want an *actionable insight*?

It is also vital to add that there is never any omen revealed to you in your cup that does not have the capability of change or transformation. There is nothing there that your free will cannot affect. This is particularly important should you receive an omen that suggests a dangerous situation or advice of a negative act against you. You can change the outcome, so do not worry.

Again, perhaps people do not act because the rational mind, our loving jailer, gives us a case of the 'fuzzies' and we conveniently forget what to do. This is why I suggest that you act on any insights you receive within 48 hours. If this is not possible, at least record what you intend to do or better still, tell a reliable friend who will keep you to it.

This book contains a simple Coffee Oracle Journal Sheet and I encourage you to use it regularly. You can photocopy it or download a version from my website www. themodernwitch.com at the Coffee Oracle section.

There, you can conveniently record the symbols your cup reveals, the meanings, your insights and the participation you are going to take. This way, you have a ready-made directions sheet to guide you through your next steps. You might even share it with a trusted friend who will remind you to follow up. It beats the 'fuzzies" every time!

the coffee oracle journal sheet

Date: _____

My Enquiry: (*insert your question*) _____

_____

coffee oracle symbols:

SYMBOL	ANATOMY OF CUP	MESSAGE

In relation to my enquiry, my interpretation is as follows: *(State what the Oracle has suggested to you)*

_____

_____

_____

_____

_____

_____

_____

my participation:

My actionable insights are as follows, and I will endeavour to act on these within a 48-hour period:

_____

_____

_____

_____

_____

_____

the 28 Day self-discovery plan
– *moving forward faster*

by now I'm presuming that you have begun to experience the benefits of the Coffee Oracle and perhaps are eager for some further insight.

Whilst a one-off reading can be incredibly useful and can be the catalyst for great change, I have always found that an extended period of work can ensure long- lasting and often permanent transformation.

With my work within the Witch's Way, I have found that profound change often occurs over a 28 day period (one moon cycle) or over what I have termed a tri-lunar cycle (that is, three moon cycles).

Within moon cycle periods, I have been privileged to see people give up smoking, heal from a dangerous illness, recover from trauma or begin to change deep-seated habits that they have tried to kick in almost every other way.

I think that when we see another force involved, one outside our own, guiding us, assisting or validating us, we decide to commit to bettering our lives or stepping up to exactly what it is that we want.

So it is because of these successes and that I am sharing a particularly successful 28-day process with you.

I call it The **28-Day Self-Discovery Plan**.

why try this?

The ancient Greek Delphic Oracle broadcast a number of special guidelines for good living that were given by the Gods to man. The first and most important of those Delphic instructions was "Know thyself".

How many of us really know our true Selves?

Perhaps even more importantly, how many of us have a good relationship with our true Selves?

If we think about some of the negative self-talk or twisted beliefs that go floating through our minds every day, and imagine saying those things out loud to a close friend, I doubt that relationship would go on much longer.

Would we indeed ever say such horrendous things to a beloved friend anyway?

I asked this question of Richard, a 42-year-old painter with a wife and two young children. Richard had trained to be an accountant and was successful at this for 15 years but decided that he wanted to follow his dream of becoming a professional artist. He had managed to support his family but he hadn't achieved the heights that he had hoped. This had resulted in his self-esteem steadily draining away and him becoming short-tempered and sulky towards his family.

"I just did not think about how much I was hating myself. When I began to notice some of my self-talk, it really validated my low self-esteem. I listened to an almost looped tape of "You are not good enough" and "You are a fraud" one day when I was due to make a pitch to a gallery. It was maddening when I thought about it," he said.

"But when you ask me to say those things to a beloved friend, I just wouldn't. How terrible. It probably wouldn't be true anyway. I would definitely be more supportive."

So wouldn't it be useful to know your true Self better and to know more about what you *really* want? Wouldn't it be great to bypass our loving jailer – the rational mind – and just be curious, just listen, just discover what it is our Self wants to say and then decisively, easily, fearlessly and joyfully act upon that conversation? Imagine how exciting and relieving that would be!

This is just what the 28-Day Self-Discovery Plan has been created for… to listen and to act.

You will find benefit from taking part in this plan if any of these statements feel true for you:

- ☕ I feel restless but I do not know why.
- ☕ I am feeling down and depressed.
- ☕ I used to feel creative but now I don't.
- ☕ I know what I have to change but I don't have the motivation.
- ☕ I have a negative behaviour that I just can't kick.
- ☕ Life should be good. I have a great job, a good family and relationship, however I feel like something is missing.
- ☕ I know I have low self-esteem.
- ☕ I wish to increase my health and vitality.
- ☕ I engage in negative self-talk.
- ☕ I am really angry/sad/resentful and I don't know why.
- ☕ I would like to build and develop my intuitive powers.
- ☕ I am at a crossroads. I am finding it hard to make a particular decision.

preparation

This is a deceptively simple program. All you need to do is commit to three things each day.

1. Have a coffee with which you will engage the Oracle.
2. Interpret and record your findings.
3. Act on any insights that you feel are necessary and important.

You will be ultilising a handy **28-Day Self-Discovery Plan** template to record all your information. It is enclosed here and is also available as a download from my website www.themodernwitch.com

You will see that the template is broken up into 28 daily entries with some additional room after each seven-day cycle and then the final 28-day period. You will record the question you ask, symbols, simple notes on your interpretation, and any actions you will take. You will find that this is a fluid process…each day spurs on the next like a domino effect.

One of the most important steps is asking the Oracle the 'right' question each day. You will find this easier to do as the days progress, but getting it 'right' over the first few days may be a little difficult.

If you are stuck on how to start, I would like you to ask one of the following broad questions:

- What do I need to know right now?
- What would you like to tell me right now?
- I want to feel better, how do I do this?

These will get the answers flowing and will give your unconscious mind a chance to speak out in all its glory. Things will start to roll after that.

an example:

Richard, our artist, decided to do the 28-Day Self-Discovery Plan. He was almost a month out from his first major painting exhibition and was racked with anxiety about whether this was the right thing to do. In fact, he was considering giving up painting all together and going back to his old nine-to-five job.

The following is his actual template and I hope it gives you some practical insight into how this process works and just how powerful it can be.

richard's 28-day self-discovery plan template

DAY	QUESTION	SYMBOL & INTERPRETATION	ACTIONABLE INSIGHTS
1	What do I need to know?	Bag on bottom of cup: rejecting gifts	I don't appreciate my talent. I knock myself.
2	What do I need to know?	Gallows: self-sabotage Jewel: precious gift	I am my own worst enemy. Be better to myself. Watch my self-talk. My artistic talent is a precious unique gift. Treat it like that. Why do I treat it otherwise?
3	What else would be good?	Apple: wisdom, learning Table: honesty	Workshops? Teaching? I should be more open and honest with myself and others. What do I want?

DAY	QUESTION	SYMBOL & INTERPRETATION	ACTIONABLE INSIGHTS
4	What would happen if I left art?	Jellyfish: directionless, purposeless	I should stick with my art, but I should extend my services. This feels good.
5	Why do I self–sabotage?	Bear: protection Tap: lack of focus	I see now that my actions are a way of self–protection. This is not helping me at all.
6	Will I change this negative behaviour?	Tunnel: hope, light Magpie: action, speed	Yes, but I must take action.
7	What do I need to do today concerning the exhibition?	Z: revolution, risks	Don't play it safe. Take the risk

Week I Summary ☕ I feel better about knowing how my bad self–talk affects me. I am aware of my purpose though and it is my art! Validation! Change the exhibition program to a more radical design.

DAY	QUESTION	SYMBOL & INTERPRETATION	ACTIONABLE INSIGHTS
8	What do I need to know?	Cage: held back, trapped, positioned at 6 o'clock	I put myself in a cage. No one else does.
9	What do I need to know?	Unicorn: creative freedom	Ha! Not trapped at all. Is creativity my key to escape?

DAY	QUESTION	SYMBOL & INTERPRETATION	ACTIONABLE INSIGHTS
10	Why do I get so angry?	Cloud: lack of clarity, seeing the negative Volcano: blowups, lack of expression	I often don't know what I want. I'm often not clear about things. I need to set intentions.
11	Why do I get angry with myself?	Mask: hiding, secrecy	I'm not honest with myself. I avoid who I am. I don't like who I am a lot of the time.
12	Why do I get so angry with my wife?	Mat: doormat, passive Turtle: feminine energy, calmness Talon: unexpected control. Who is controlling whom?	Really? Do I treat her that badly? Discuss issues and behaviour with my wife. Apologise to her. Ask her what she wants.
13	What can I do about the anger?	Bridge: finding common ground Bride: commit and change	I need to build a bridge to peace. I need to surrender my control issues. I want to change and commit to this.
14	What do I need to know?	Tunnel: hope	Things will improve.

Week 2 Summary ☕ Wow, big week! Set clear intentions for myself. Discuss things with my family. Relax. Take wife and kids on a holiday next month after exhibition.

DAY	QUESTION	SYMBOL & INTERPRETATION	ACTIONABLE INSIGHTS
15	What do I need to know?	Baby: fresh starts new ideas. Barrow: burdens lifted	Things are changing. I'm on the right track. I notice I am not so angry.
16	What do I need to know?	Gate: an entrance	The exhibition will be the entrance to new things; I will put all my heart into it. I will stop worrying.
17	What do I need to know about the exhibition?	Jar: storing something precious Oar: team work	I should honour myself and mark this occasion somehow. Involve my wife.
18	What do I need to know?	Oar: again! More team work	I met with the gallery today and there were some loose ends I may have missed if I didn't go.
19	What do I need to do to be happy?	Map: destination, finding a way, direction	Doing this plan is a start, but I need to have a set of intentions to work and live by. A life map.
20	What do I need to know?	Umbrella: protection	Good to know I'm being watched over and have support.
21	What do I need to know?	Map: this Oracle is persistent!	Plan out some intentions for next year.

Week 3 Summary ☕ I feel really determined and refreshed. More organised. Looking forward to the exhibition more.

DAY	QUESTION	SYMBOL & INTERPRETATION	ACTIONABLE INSIGHTS
22	How will the exhibition be received?	Throne: kingly success	This exhibition will be great.
23	Will my exhibition be a success?	Genie: good surprises, wishes granted	I'm sending out an intention that my work be a success and really be seen!
24	What do I need to know?	Sign of Virgo: perfectionism vs. excellence?	I think I want to do a great job but sometimes that spills out into perfectionism, which stops the creative process. I need to be aware of this.
25	What do I need to know?	Bell: announcements	Good media?
26	Why I am suddenly scared?	Trumpet: recognition, announcements The number 2: change, home	I'm afraid of success. How will it change things? How will my home life be affected? There are strategies to deal with this.

DAY	QUESTION	SYMBOL & INTERPRETATION	ACTIONABLE INSIGHTS
27	The exhibition is tonight. What do I need to know?	Flying bird: happiness, freedom	Exhibition was a great success. Great media reviews. That bell was right! I'm happy!
28	What do I need to know that I don't already know?	Oak: stability, strength	If I continue on this way, it will be good for all aspects of my life. Security for my family, yet freedom for me.

my key findings:

I know that art is my purpose but I can extend my work into other areas such as teaching. I need to express my self more. I feel better now that I have set some clear intentions. I feel like I have got to the source of my anger and now I can do something about it.

my key actionable insights which i promise to enact immediately:

Begin to organise a workshop to test the waters. Book a holiday for me and the family with some of the profit from my exhibition. Ask my wife to help me stay on track for my intentions and Life Map. Listen more. Be confident in my gifts. Keep working, without being affected by unhealthy doubts.

By reading Richard's template, I'm sure you can see how easily the Oracle was able to lead Richard in the best direction for self knowledge and actualisation.

Note that sometimes, he was surprised or challenged by what the Oracle said, but in the same vein he was willing to act upon the advice the best way he knew how. Acting on insights is vital to the success of the discovery process. It gives you the personal momentum to change course if necessary and move with the flow and not against it.

At time of writing, Richard is now preparing for his second solo exhibition. He can't believe that he ever considered dropping his art for his old corporate life.

"This 28-Day Plan was as easy as grabbing a coffee, but gave me some really complex things to think about. Bottom-line, though, it gave me both confidence in my own talents and decision–making abilities and this has had benefits way beyond that one month," Richard said.

"I'm still working on some issues, like my bad temper, but at least I know why I react that way and this insight gives me hints on how to recover from this. Honestly, I am not really into this 'Oracle stuff' but it worked for me!"

I invite you to allow the power of the Coffee Oracle to work for you too. Print out a copy of the following template, buy yourself a coffee and start now! Knowing thyself has never been easier.

using the symbol dictionary – read this first!

By now, you have learnt the importance of using your own powerful intuition to piece together the puzzle of the Oracle.

Following, you will find hundreds of symbols in alphabetical order. Each entry features Key Messages and The Oracle Says, which is the Oracular message. Some entries show Additional Insights if there is extra information that is important to know.

the entries:

☕ *Key Messages:* These are the core concepts pertaining to each Oracle symbol. It is important to take all of these concepts into account whilst considering the meaning of your particular message. Naturally though, one or two will 'ring true' for you and this will form the guidance you have received.

☕ *The Oracle Says:* This message features vital thought-starters. This section should provide triggers for your intuition and enticements for your deeper unconscious. The Oracle may ask a question of you, challenge you, or remind you of something long lost. This message is often a more spiritual one and is important to consider when weaving your enquiry together with your symbols.

☕ *Additional Insights:* These are extra pieces of information that may further impact your reading. I have gathered these insights after decades of Oracle work and literally thousands of cups of coffee. Often they will mention an unusual or unexpected result of identifying that particular symbol, the effects of it combined with other symbols or a description of its shadow or negative aspect. Not all symbol entries contain additional insights, but if your chosen symbol does, please remember to take it into consideration.

some handy hints:

- Relax! One of the greatest barriers to successful Oracle reading is fear. Many people get worried or tense that they will 'get it wrong' somehow and so make an inaccurate interpretation with seemingly dire consequences! There is no wrong or right here as long as you connect with your inner Self. The best way to do that is to relax, breathe and think of something pleasant.

  I like to approach a reading with a happy sense of curiosity and discovery. "I wonder what I will discover today?" This certainly takes the pressure off!

- If you have no specific question to ask, a question like, "What is it that I need to know?" makes for an interesting and provocative Coffee Oracle reading.

- If your symbol is slightly confusing visually and you aren't sure what it might be, (yes, sometimes a pear can look like an avocado), feel free to consult a number of entries. Then decide which one seems more relevant and 'right' for you. Again, this is a way of building your intuitive skills.

- If you discover an animal in your cup that isn't featured in the Symbol Dictionary, I have added an additional Animal Guides list in the Resources section at the rear of the book.

- Remember: After identifying your Oracle symbols you must lay these over the Anatomy of your cup. This gives deeper information pertaining to timing and distance, for example. This will increase the detail and accuracy of your reading.

- Should you find a symbol in your cup that isn't featured here you might try to work out its meaning yourself. Alternatively feel free to email me your query at Stacey@themodernwitch.com. I will keep a record of these symbols we discover together and add them to the next edition!

☕ Should you see absolutely nothing in your cup, look again. If there still isn't anything, try again in a little while with another cup. Usually we see nothing in the cup because the force of our rational conscious mind is too strong. Relax! It's time to allow your imagination and intuition to run free!

☕ The more often you consult the Coffee Oracle, the more comfortable you will be at this process and the easier and more enjoyable it will be. You will quickly become familiar with all the symbols and their meanings and the interpretation process will flow much more quickly. My recommendation is to do a reading with your daily cup of coffee for the first week or so to get the 'hang of things'. I promise you will love it!

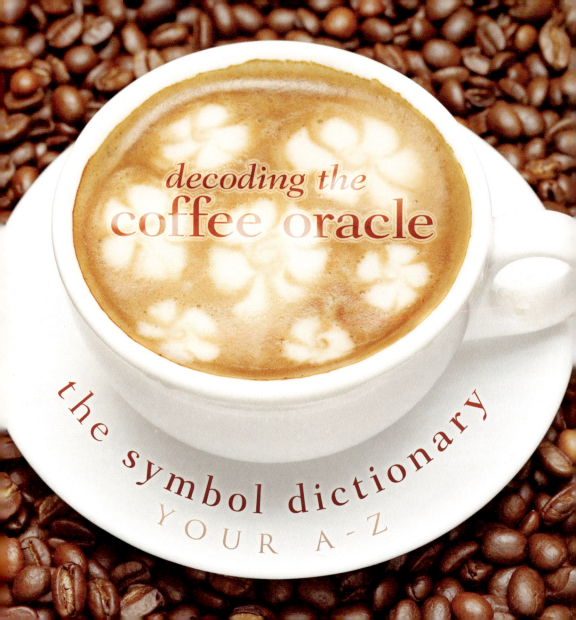

decoding the coffee oracle

the symbol dictionary
YOUR A-Z

☕ ACE

KEY MESSAGES: winning, triumph in competition, strategic thinking

THE ORACLE SAYS: Through careful planning and great thinking you will come up a winner. This win may surprise others, and will earn you greater respect.

ADDITIONAL INSIGHTS: An Ace on the bottom of your cup may indicate your competitor may have an unexpected advantage, so you may wish to rethink your own strategy. Aces may appear with other card–related symbols like Clubs, Hearts, Diamonds, and Spades. Refer to these symbols further in the Dictionary.

☕ ACORN

KEY MESSAGES: growth, from something small something larger is developed, thrift, planning

THE ORACLE SAYS: From the tiny acorn the mighty oak tree grows. Trust that your project, idea or relationship will grow from humble beginnings into something magnificent. Slow but steady growth is indicated.

☕ ALIEN

KEY MESSAGES: the unknown, new places and people, feeling 'alienated'

THE ORACLE SAYS: Whether or not you believe in alternate life forms, feeling like an alien in your own territory is often an unsettling experience. Knowing that being 'different' is ultimately one of the things that makes us powerful is an important lesson. Alternatively, welcoming the unknown by courting new people, places and experiences often blows the dust off an ordinary life.

♨ ALLIGATOR

KEY MESSAGES: secrets, booby traps, all is not what it seems, old ways

THE ORACLE SAYS: There are some secrets that need to be exposed in order for wise decisions to be made. Look into the details of the situation and investigate the issue from all possible angles. Do not trust that the waters are calm and benign.

♨ ALMOND

KEY MESSAGES: purity, goodness

THE ORACLE SAYS: There is no ulterior motive or negative intent in the situation or person you are seeking guidance for. There is an innocence in the wishes of another towards you, even though it may feel otherwise.

♨ AEROPLANE

KEY MESSAGES: travel by air, escape, hopes

THE ORACLE SAYS: A journey by air is approaching and will be of significance to you. Do you feel the need right now to escape your current situation? Would a change of scenery refresh you? Act now and book yourself a ticket.

ADDITIONAL INSIGHTS: If the aeroplane is flying upwards towards the rim, your hopes for something will be fulfilled. If the plane is facing downwards or sits at the bottom of the cup, be ready for disappointment.

ANCHOR

KEY MESSAGES: security, holding oneself back or to one place

THE ORACLE SAYS: It is good to feel secure and stable if you have been experiencing the storms of life. All is well. However, if you are feeling weighed down by a person or a situation, particularly at work, it may now be time to pull up the anchor, chart new territory and set sail.

ANGEL

KEY MESSAGES: inspiration, safety, protection, assurance

THE ORACLE SAYS: If you have been worried about an issue or have been dogged by lack of creativity or hope, rest assured this will now change.

ADDITIONAL INSIGHTS: If the angel is at the very top of the cup, assistance is being offered right now or there is someone close to you who can help with your problem.

☕ ANKH

KEY MESSAGES: long life, creativity, renewal, soul

THE ORACLE SAYS: There is more to think about than what you see. Look beyond what your eyes capture and listen to your soul. No problem is insurmountable. A time for renewal is at hand.

☕ ANT

KEY MESSAGES: teamwork, triumph of small over big, friendship

THE ORACLE SAYS: There is no need to do this on your own. This is a time to enlist the help of friends or a team of people. Although the problem looks vast and complex, it is not and a solution can be found by breaking it down into components.

☕ ANTELOPE

KEY MESSAGES: freedom, speed, agility, physicality

THE ORACLE SAYS: Freedom is not just a state of mind but also a physical need. When was the last time you allowed your body to truly stretch out or run wildly…even for just 30 seconds? Feeling the power of your own physicality celebrates your body as the powerful miracle that it is.

ADDITIONAL INSIGHTS: An antelope near the handle of your cup (or in the 3o'clock position) means that the time is right for an immediate physical change. For example: moving house, altering your diet, getting fitter.

☕ ANTENNA

KEY MESSAGES: finding one's way, tuning in to what is around and within

THE ORACLE SAYS: You are now beginning to open your heart and mind to a new paradigm of thinking and acting. You have been inspired by others who have gone before you but probably not your family. Keep discovering and learning by watching.

☕ APPLE

KEY MESSAGES: teaching and knowledge, new beginnings, a temptation, an opportunity, good health, computers

THE ORACLE SAYS: It is now time to open your eyes to new opportunities and new ways of learning. Learning and teaching are both as important as each other.

ADDITIONAL INSIGHTS: At the bottom of the cup, seeing an apple means a temptation or that an opportunity is there for the taking. Act quickly.

☕ AQUARIUS (symbol is two wavy water lines)

KEY MESSAGES: a person born under the sign Aquarius may be important to you (21st January and 19th February), friendship, new ideas, revolution and innovation

THE ORACLE SAYS: Innovation and a fresh way of looking at things are important in the short term. Revolutionary thinking is needed.

☕ ARC

KEY MESSAGES: a project or intention will be successful or may fail depending on the shape of the arc

THE ORACLE SAYS: Look closely at the shape of the arc. Is it leaning upwards to success or downwards warning of a less than satisfactory result? Heed the insight and act accordingly.

ADDITIONAL INSIGHTS: An arc at the bottom of a coffee cup signifies life after death.

☕ ARCH

KEY MESSAGES: unexpected journey, a project will be completed successfully, permanency from something temporary

THE ORACLE SAYS: Do not worry. The beginning you have made will not be for nothing. There will be an ending that will please you.

☕ ARIES (symbol is two curved goat horns)

KEY MESSAGES: a person born under the sign of Aries (21st March – 20th April) endurance

THE ORACLE SAYS: Stamina and endurance will enable you to triumph in this situation.

☕ ARM

KEY MESSAGES: assistance is available, love and protection, partnership

THE ORACLE SAYS: There is nothing more supportive than an arm encircling you in love or compassion. Know that you are supported and that help is there for the asking.

☕ ARMY

KEY MESSAGES: organised protest, gaining support

THE ORACLE SAYS: You have a job ahead in organising your support or having your voice heard. Gather your generals, your officers, your ground troops and ensure that you get input from all levels before you proceed with the 'plan' or 'attack'.

☕ ARROW

KEY MESSAGES: focus, true aim, being on target, clarity

THE ORACLE SAYS: The Universe is signaling that it is time to clarify your intention and move forward with a solid goal. If you have done this, the arrow signifies that you are on target and on your way.

ADDITIONAL INSIGHTS: Arrows pointing downwards can indicate unfocussed intention or the need to clarify instructions or issues.

☕ AUTOMOBILE

KEY MESSAGES: sexual liberation, pace of life, a change of scenery

THE ORACLE SAYS: What kind of car do you see? Is it a racing car or an old classic? Whether it is something fast and furious or slow and steady, it's a symbol asking you to alter the pace of life. The car also symbolises a new sense of freedom and liberation with sexual matters and asks for a new level of trust in relationships.

☕ AVOCADO

KEY MESSAGES: feminine care and support, sexual maturity, fertility

THE ORACLE SAYS: There is great feminine power around you right now, and this presence will grant you deep and long-lasting support. The sacred power of the divine feminine grants you creativity and a life-force virtually vibrating with potential.

ADDITIONAL INSIGHTS: A very common symbol when a young woman first enters sexual maturity or just prior to a baby being conceived.

 AXE

KEY MESSAGES: freedom by cutting through what no longer serves you, male sexual power, female sexual intent

THE ORACLE SAYS: There are behaviors or situations that no longer serve you. By identifying and removing these elements, you will find greater freedom and joy in your life. Be honest in your relationships, particularly those of a sexual nature.

☕ BABY

KEY MESSAGES: a birth, new ideas/business, fresh starts

THE ORACLE SAYS: Here is your opportunity to start afresh or to be confident in the new ideas and concepts that you have thought of. Move forward with these and manifest them mightily! This new birth will bring you great happiness and satisfaction, although there will have to be an investment of significant time and effort.

ADDITIONAL INSIGHTS: Should you spot a baby close to the rim of your cup, a baby will soon grace your life, whether it is through your own pregnancy or that of another. If the baby should appear at the bottom of the cup, the omen is not so joyous. This means that a physical pregnancy may be in doubt or that the new idea may fail. Remember though, we are never shown anything that cannot be changed or influenced through action.

☕ BAG

KEY MESSAGES: carrying, gifts, receiving/rejecting

THE ORACLE SAYS: There may be a heavy burden that you carry or emotions that weight heavily upon you such as guilt or regret. It is being suggested that you drop this bag and reduce your load. Work through these issues and peace will be restored.

ADDITIONAL INSIGHTS: Should you see a bag in your cup that is sealed tightly, you will either reject a proposal put to you or an offer that you post will be refused. If the bag is open however, expect the opposite. A gift will be forthcoming.

 **BALL**

KEY MESSAGES: playful, bounce, chasing, physical exercise

THE ORACLE SAYS: Perhaps you are feeling that life has thrown you a curve ball. Perhaps right now you are chasing your tail or have little time for play. However, the Oracle indicates that these things have been the downwards trajectory of an upwards bounce. Things will and are already improving, but you have to have the eyes to see this.

ADDITIONAL INSIGHTS: If you can recognise a particular type of ball eg: football, baseball, this may be an instruction to take up that sport or that someone who plays that sport will soon become significant in your life.

BALLOON

KEY MESSAGES: celebration, surprise, unexpected events

THE ORACLE SAYS: If you see a balloon floating around the upper half of your cup, a sudden turn of events will surprise you in a positive way. This will most probably be around money, career or business. If the balloon is hovering around the bottom half of your cup, the surprise may not be so pleasant or the project you are working on may take a longer time than expected to get of the ground.

ADDITIONAL INSIGHTS: A number of balloons normally indicate a party or big celebration.

☕ BANANA

KEY MESSAGES: romance, tropical locale, mistakes

THE ORACLE SAYS: For those who are seeking a healthy relationship, this omen suggests that within three months you should find it. For those already attached, there will be heightened levels of connection and intimacy.

ADDITIONAL INSIGHTS: If you find a banana on the bottom of your cup, be mindful or your attention to detail or your concentration level. You may be set for a 'slip up!'

☕ BAND

KEY MESSAGES: music, co-operation, synergy

THE ORACLE SAYS: If you see a band of musicians in your cup you are seeing an invitation to exercise more cooperation and team work in your family and career life. You will encounter more success and happiness should you make a conscious effort to connect with the power of many.

☕ BANDIT

KEY MESSAGES: warning, robbing, escape, negative intentions

THE ORACLE SAYS: Be warned that there may be someone who is intent upon robbing you of either your self-respect, your reputation or something more material. This omen is not sent to worry you unnecessarily, just to encourage you to place your focus on your Self and your intentions and to only allow what you desire into your life.

☕ BARREL

KEY MESSAGES: wealth, socialising, happiness

THE ORACLE SAYS: A barrel in your cup is a wonderful omen indicating great prosperity, good health and a strong network of friends which all bring you great happiness.

ADDITIONAL INSIGHTS: A broken or leaking barrel indicates loss of money, profit or reputation.

☕ BARROW

KEY MESSAGES: movement, burdens lifted, involvement, the garden

THE ORACLE SAYS: If you have been feeling stagnant and restless, this will be alleviated shortly. You are also encouraged to 'get your hands' dirty to resolve a problem. You may also feel relief from stress by connecting with nature. Why not go for a bush walk or even do a spot of gardening?

 BAT

KEY MESSAGES: good fortune, night time, happy visit

THE ORACLE SAYS: In many animist spiritual practices, the visit of a bat indicates an increase in prosperity and the arrival of a visitor that brings great happiness to the family. For some of us in Western cultures, the bat has become a symbol of evil and darkness, which is an incorrect mutation of old lore.

ADDITIONAL INSIGHTS: If there is more than one bat in your cup, expect good fortune to swoop upon you quickly or to achieve your goals in a shorter period of time than you anticipated.

BATH

KEY MESSAGES: cleansing, relaxation, relief, revitalise

THE ORACLE SAYS: Your worries will wash away. Have faith that the Universe will provide for you and that all things will be as you have asked. Your worries will reduce considerably very soon.

ADDITIONAL INSIGHTS: If the bath is at the bottom of the cup, this could indicate a financial loss in the short term.

BEAD

KEY MESSAGES: connection, love, friends, exchange

THE ORACLE SAYS: You are being urged to make a fair exchange. Perhaps you are not being paid a fair salary, or on the other hand are not offering one. Perhaps the issue is spending enough time or connecting fully with those that you love. Ensure there is balance in all your dealings.

ADDITIONAL INSIGHTS: If the beads are very close together or strung together like a necklace, this indicates that the people closest to you will unite for a purpose. Also see the entry 'Necklace'.

BED

KEY MESSAGES: sexual satisfaction, marriage, rest, peace/anxiety

THE ORACLE SAYS: Our beds are meant to be a place of safety, sanctuary and delight. Seeing one in your cup is a warm and happy omen displaying a tendency for wonderful sexual experiences and a peaceful demeanor in the future.

ADDITIONAL INSIGHTS: If the bed looks broken or the sheets are messy, sleepless nights are what is indicated. You are urged to seek out the nature of your anxiety and solve it once and for all.

 BEE

KEY MESSAGES: groups of people, word of mouth, buzz/gossip

THE ORACLE SAYS: Just as the bee goes pollinating from flower to flower, so will your message reach large groups of people simply by word of mouth or from an initial few. On the flip side of this, be aware that negative messages such as gossip can also spread this way, so be mindful of your intentions and behavior.

ADDITIONAL INSIGHTS: A bee at the bottom of the cup can indicate malicious gossip or unemployment.

BEEHIVE

KEY MESSAGES: money, prosperity, reward

THE ORACLE SAYS: All your hard work will now be rewarded. Like a beehive hums with activity, so will your office, mind or place of work. The rewards will be sweet.

☕ BELL

KEY MESSAGES: attention, announcements, a wedding

THE ORACLE SAYS: You will soon receive significant news which will have some important long-term consequences for you. You are also being invited to pay closer attention to some aspect of business or to a legal issue, which may disrupt the positive flow of things if ignored.

☕ BELT

KEY MESSAGES: overindulgence, money, food, support

THE ORACLE SAYS: Are you over compensating for something by overindulging? Too much shopping, eating, drinking or working means that there is a unmet need which gives you pain and that you are covering by these 'too much' behaviours. Know that you are supported and that you can safely reduce this compulsion.

☕ BIKE (also see Motorbike)

KEY MESSAGES: movement, better/worse, simplicity

THE ORACLE SAYS: If you see a bike in your cup, this indicates progressive movement, however this movement can be forward, backward, down or up depending upon the direction of the bike in your cup. Generally, this omen heralds a call for greater simplicity in all your dealings, in particular, the kind of lifestyle you are living. This will lead to greater happiness.

☕ BILLIARDS

KEY MESSAGES: competition, strategy, venue where billiards are played, billiard player

THE ORACLE SAYS: Prepare yourself for some stiff competition, but the challenge will most probably be a pleasurable one. You may face more than one opponent.

☕ BIRD (also see Swallow)

KEY MESSAGES: happiness, news, luck

THE ORACLE SAYS: Should you see a bird winging its way across the expanse of your cup, the omen is all good. Traditionally birds were the bringers of news and of good fortune. Particularly, a bird in full flight indicates dazzling good luck and great happiness.

ADDITIONAL INSIGHTS: Typically, a flock of birds means great conversation or innovative team work. Different birds have different attributes so check the Animal Guide chart in the Resources section to gain more insight.

☕ BIRD'S NEST

KEY MESSAGES: security, parental or sibling love, saving

THE ORACLE SAYS: A bird's nest appearing in your cup indicates solid family love, support and love. A nest also emphasises the importance of having a secure sanctuary and trust with those close to you. Financially, a nest indicates an intention or a need to save money for the future. If the nest contains eggs, additions to the family or some brilliant new ideas are indicated.

ADDITIONAL INSIGHTS: If the nest is broken or badly formed, this normally indicates either a breakdown in the family such as a divorce or the need to invest more wisely.

☕ BOAT (also see Ship)

KEY MESSAGES: validity, success

THE ORACLE SAYS: If a small boat floats around your cup know that you will certainly get to your goal, slowly but surely. If the boat has no leaks or is not being buffeted by any negative symbols, your current course of action is the right one.

☕ BOMB

KEY MESSAGES: ignorance, facing facts, explosiveness

THE ORACLE SAYS: A situation has been ticking away for some time and you have either not known or acknowledged this. The situation will become extremely explosive for all involved if things are not acknowledged and action taken. It is recommended that you disarm the situation as soon as possible

BONE

KEY MESSAGES: basics, raw, facts, past influences, tenacity

THE ORACLE SAYS: You are being advised to get down to the bare bones of the issue. Simplicity and taking just the facts into account will help solve the problem. You may also be like a 'dog with a bone' and be showing extreme tenacity or even stubbornness over an issue. Also, the appearance of bones may indicate past hurts or old loves which are influencing you actions at this time.

ADDITIONAL INSIGHTS: If the bones look like a pirate's crossed bones, with or without the skull, it means you are being warned about something. Check the other symbols in your cup for clues.

BOOK

KEY MESSAGES: wisdom, reading, secrecy/openness

THE ORACLE SAYS: Open your mind to new discoveries and learning. No matter how old you are, you still must be open to the gathering of wisdom.

ADDITIONAL INSIGHTS: Is the book opened? This indicates honesty and that there is nothing to hide. Is the book closed? This indicates that all is not being displayed and there may be secrets that are not being revealed to you.

☕ BOOMERANG

KEY MESSAGES: return, karma

THE ORACLE SAYS: You will return to a place you have visited previously. The friend that you think you have lost will return. The opportunity that has slipped through your fingers will not truly be lost. The actions that you take right now do have consequences that will turn back to you.

☕ BOOT

KEY MESSAGES: journey, hard work, protection, change

THE ORACLE SAYS: Pulling on your boots is a little like rolling up your sleeves in that hard work and concentrated effort is needed. A pair of boots normally indicates travel over land.

ADDITIONAL INSIGHTS: What do the boots actually look like? If the boot is a workman's boot you may be destined to do some renovation or meet someone who is involved in a trade. If they look like cowboy boots, perhaps a trip to the country is in order or you may find that someone from a farm becomes important to you. If the boot sits at the bottom of the cup you may suffer a rejection.

☕ BOTTLE

KEY MESSAGES: temptation, isolation, alcohol/liquids

THE ORACLE SAYS: There may be a lucrative offer made to you and you will be tempted to take it. Before doing so, check the ethics of the situation and ensure that you have an exit strategy. Someone who works with bottles such as a sommelier, winemaker, or a milkman will be significant in your near future.

ADDITIONAL INSIGHTS: A bottle at the bottom of your cup indicates that you may be isolated from something or someone you enjoy if you do not change the way you are behaving. A broken bottle indicates someone who has failed with a new venture or someone who has a problem with alcohol.

☕ **BOW** (as in a ribbon tied into a bow)

KEY MESSAGE: gift, ease, youth

THE ORACLE SAYS: The Universe is ready to bestow a gift upon you that you have wanted for some time. Know that you have co-created this gift and there is more to come if you continue the same way. There is no need to struggle; the thing you want will now come to you quickly and easily.

☕ **BOW** (as in bow and arrow)

KEY MESSAGES: ancient wisdom, force, intention, focus, protection

THE ORACLE SAYS: In some ancient cultures the bow (and arrow) became a protective symbol and one that encompassed the ideals of wisdom, ethics and focused spirituality. A bow also indicates the need for clear intentions in order to reach your target.

ADDITIONAL INSIGHTS: If the bow is on the bottom of the cup, there is a need to put up your shield somewhat. You may need protection.

BOWL

KEY MESSAGES: women's magic, receiving, allowing, creation, transformation

THE ORACLE SAYS: Allow yourself to be nourished by receiving rather than giving. No one can continue to give indefinitely without feeling drained and broken. Allow yourself to fully accept the love, attention, rest or opportunities that are being offered. A bowl placed near the rim of the cup, encourages women to discover and extend their personal power. It is recommended that you 'refill your bowl' by communing in nature or spending time with other women.

BRA

KEY MESSAGES: maternal support, sex, fantasies

THE ORACLE SAYS: A bra appearing in your cup normally signifies that assistance or support can be found from the maternal line of the family.

ADDITIONAL INSIGHTS: If the bra is on the bottom of the cup it urges you to reduce the time you spend fantasising about sex and sexual matters.

BRACELET

KEY MESSAGES: innocent love, romance, affection

THE ORACLE SAYS: If you see a bracelet circling your cup, it indicates a sweet and innocent romantic love that is free from baser desires. There is a strong friendship and affection that may or may not lead to a full-blown love. If you are hoping for a commitment from a suitor, this is not an engagement ring!

BRANCH

KEY MESSAGES: growth, fertility, renewal, peace

THE ORACLE SAYS: What you thought would never grow, will. What you had little faith in will be reborn. The work you have already completed will not be wasted, although the project will change drastically.

ADDITIONAL INSIGHTS: A branch being carried by a bird signifies peace and reconciliation.

☕ BRIDE

KEY MESSAGES: marriage, commitment, change

THE ORACLE SAYS: In many cultures, getting married meant a new home, a new family and often a complete lifestyle change. Similarly, seeing a bride in your cup means that you will be experiencing major change. Do not be afraid of this nor resist it. You have asked for a better life and this change is necessary for it to manifest.

☕ BRIDGE

KEY MESSAGES: finding similarities, journey, change

THE ORACLE SAYS: You will be asked to build a bridge between two disparate philosophies, people or businesses. Your objective will be to find the points of similarity rather than emphasise the rather obvious points of difference. Both parties can win here with only smart, small adjustments. A bridge often signifies a journey, and this can be a spiritual or a physical one.

☕ BROOM

KEY MESSAGES: cleansing, fertility, change

THE ORACLE SAYS: Witches use their brooms (besoms) to clear away energies that no longer are of value to them and a broom in your cup heralds the same type of change. It is truly time to clean up your act. There are patterns and behaviours that no longer serve you. There may be people around you that really do not support you. Your home or workplace may not be what you need. Sweep clean your life!

ADDITIONAL INSIGHTS: A broom at the rim of your cup signifies great fertility. This can be referring to fertility of ideas of money or of course, your physical fertility.

BRUSH

KEY MESSAGES: appearance, discovery, first impressions

THE ORACLE SAYS: They say that you only get one chance to make a first impression. Whether that is true or not, you are being asked to focus on just that and matters of your appearance. Are you happy with the impression you give others about yourself? Is this impression aligned with your true and authentic self? Do you feel as though the real you does not shine through to others adequately?

BUCKET

KEY MESSAGES: money, good fortune

THE ORACLE SAYS: You will attract a sizeable salary increase or monetary gain. This most likely will be in the form of a bonus or one-off payment.

☕ BULL

KEY MESSAGES: strength, honour, masculine power, a Taurean

THE ORACLE SAYS: If a male finds a bull in his cup, it is urging him to reacquaint himself with the attributes of masculine power. These include but are not limited to strength, protection, honour, ethics and action. If it is a female reading the cup she is encouraged to put her trust in a man who is demonstrates these attributes or develop a healthy balance of these within herself.

ADDITIONAL INSIGHTS: If the bull is surrounded by symbols indicating money or numbers, the advice here is to be 'bullish' in any investment or financial decisions. This means move forward and do not hold back. A bull at the bottom of the cup may indicate a temper that is too easily enraged.

☕ BUG (see Insect)

☕ BUSH

KEY MESSAGES: hidden/obvious, signal, new horizons

THE ORACLE SAYS: A bush normally indicates either something is absolutely obvious, but you are not seeing it or it is a very strong signal to move forward. One of the most famous natural Oracles was the Bible's famous burning bush which was an unmistakable sign.

☕ BUTTERFLY

KEY MESSAGES: transformation, spiritual messenger, new beginnings, freedom, flightiness, prayer

THE ORACLE SAYS: Many cultures believe that butterflies are the carriers of messages from humans to Gods. Whisper your intention or wish to a butterfly and she will fly directly to the ear of the Goddess. Butterflies are also omens of transformation. Things will change readily for you if you so wish it. There may well be a period of chaos but, naturally, this will pass.

ADDITIONAL INSIGHTS: A butterfly at the bottom of your cup may signify a flighty person who cannot be trusted.

☕ CACTUS

KEY MESSAGES: Living through difficult circumstances, stamina, late bloom

THE ORACLE SAYS: Although your goal may seem far away, you have the courage to endure the time it takes for it to bloom and come into fruition.

☕ CAGE

KEY MESSAGES: frustration, being held back or apart, lack of freedom, claustrophobia

THE ORACLE SAYS: Your freedom is at stake. How long are you willing to be caged and frustrated, whether it is spiritually, creatively or physically? You can take steps to free yourself from the situation. There is always a choice.

ADDITIONAL INSIGHTS: If the cage seems to have an open door or very wide bars, it signifies you have begun to experience your freedom again by stepping away from whatever binds you.

☕ CAKE

KEY MESSAGES: riches and prosperity, a celebration, a birthday

THE ORACLE SAYS: Let your hair down, it's time to celebrate! There is an occasion to celebrate coming up in the near future. It will most likely be associated with prosperity or richness in family life.

☕ CAMEL

KEY MESSAGES: endurance, a lengthy journey, exotic travel

THE ORACLE SAYS: Prepare yourself for a journey that will be lengthy and interesting. Although you may feel trepidation, fear not, you have the endurance and the innate abilities to not just survive, but thrive.

ADDITIONAL INSIGHTS: If the camel appears upside down or seated, expect delays to a project. If the camel has two humps it indicates the need to be prepared for a protracted project with a resolution some time off.

☕ CANCER (the astrological symbol is a crab)

KEY MESSAGES: Someone born between 22nd June and 23rd July will be prominent in your life, matters of the home.

THE ORACLE SAYS: Look to your home and those in it. Direct your efforts towards your property, your garden, or finding that special place that feels like home.

☕ CANDLE

KEY MESSAGES: hope, inspiration, illumination, learning

THE ORACLE SAYS: There is a wise old saying: "Better to light a candle than to curse the darkness". Inspiration is within you. Ensure you only surround yourself with those people who support you. Your situation is not fixed, but changeable. Hope abounds.

ADDITIONAL INSIGHTS: A candle with the wick showing with no flame signifies an idea that you have not put into practice yet…and should!

CAPRICORN (the astrological symbol is a goat)

KEY MESSAGES: Someone born between 22nd December and 20th January will feature strongly in your life, ambition, isolation

THE ORACLE SAYS: Having ambition in life is a positive thing, but it must be balanced – neither too much drive nor too little. Too much leads to a dangerous single–mindedness and isolation. Too little breeds fear and confusion.

CAR (see Automobile)

CARROT

KEY MESSAGES: a fresh approach, male potency, great health

THE ORACLE SAYS: It's time to enjoy the strength and high energy a well functioning body provides. Sparkling good health and a fresh approach on all things physical is indicated. If you are male, a new sexual partner or improvement in your current sexual relationship is likely.

CASTLE

KEY MESSAGES: royalty, protection, wealth, upward movement

THE ORACLE SAYS: You will be soon enjoying a positive change to your financial situation or status and this will be a long-term change for the better. If you are about to purchase a home or are saving for one, you will find a property that will be a true sanctuary for you.

ADDITIONAL INSIGHTS: If a castle appears on the bottom of the cup or it looks in ruins, it may signify that a period of peace or prosperity is about to be broken. Investigate the other symbols in the cup for more clarity.

CAT

KEY MESSAGES: independence, confidence, improved luck, feminine sexual power

THE ORACLE SAYS: Displaying confidence about your decision will make all the difference. Listen to your own counsel and if necessary 'go it alone'. There is enormous power in the feminine way and you ignore this at your peril. If you are a woman, you are being guided to re-examine your attitude to sex and power.

☕ CAULDRON

KEY MESSAGES: synergy, bringing disparate elements together, change

THE ORACLE SAYS: Imagine putting the ingredients for a stew in a pot. Each ingredient changes and transforms as it interacts with heat and the other ingredients. Likewise, it is time for you to transform yourself and your situation. Look at all the elements in your life right now and see how they can be synergistically recombined or transformed into the life you want.

ADDITIONAL INSIGHTS: If there is a cauldron at the bottom of your cup it is time to re-examine the past for clues on how to make your future more to your liking.

☕ CHAIN

KEY MESSAGES: linking, devotion/entrapment

THE ORACLE SAYS: A chain must be read carefully. In its most positive sense, a chain can signify a strong connection and a loving devotion. In its most negative aspect, a chain indicates entrapment, a smothering relationship and no room to move.

ADDITIONAL INSIGHTS: A chain with missing links or completely broken, indicates a flaw in a plan or that a relationship will soon end.

☕ CHAMPAGNE BOTTLE/GLASS

KEY MESSAGES: celebration, triumph, winning, socialising

THE ORACLE SAYS: Allow the joyous nature of celebration to permeate your mind and body and refresh your spirit. You will achieve the intention that you have set, so do not worry.

☕ CHICKEN

KEY MESSAGES: home, family, new outlook

THE ORACLE SAYS: Home and your family should take precedence right now. There may be a new birth in the family. If you are feeling slightly jaded right now, look to your beliefs. It may be time for a new view on things.

☕ CHILLI

KEY MESSAGES: life will be 'hotting up', fiery personality, speedy conclusion

THE ORACLE SAYS: Welcome more heat and passion into your life. If projects and relationships have been stagnant they will soon heat up. A decision will now be made promptly.

CIRCLE

KEY MESSAGES: a natural conclusion, a marriage/partnership, a holistic view

THE ORACLE SAYS: Nature adores a full circle and you should know that things will come to an effortless natural conclusion very soon. You, or someone close to you, may be welcoming in a new partner or receiving a marriage proposal.

CLIFF

KEY MESSAGES: stop now, take careful assessment before progressing, be prepared

THE ORACLE SAYS: Take a breath and do not proceed with your endeavor until you are sure you have taken every detail and consequence into consideration. You are being warned to be very prepared before you leap forward.

CLOCK

KEY MESSAGES: timing is important, running out of time

THE ORACLE SAYS: There is a right time for everything and although patience is often called for, this is not the case here. Seeing a clock in your cup means that time is of the essence and action is necessary.

ADDITIONAL INSIGHTS: A clock at the bottom of the cup suggests that you may have missed the opportunity – time has run out. You now have a chance to rethink and recreate.

☕ CLOUD

KEY MESSAGES: trouble ahead, misunderstanding, lack of clarity

THE ORACLE SAYS: Allow nothing to cloud your judgment on a current issue. Get the facts. Misunderstandings may happen easily and may cause unnecessary trouble.

ADDITIONAL INSIGHTS: A dark looking cloud with a light outline means that there is a benefit to a situation that seems completely negative. Yes, clouds can have a silver lining!

☕ CLOVER

KEY MESSAGES: good luck (particularly if it's a four leafed clover), an easy path, the Trinity (maiden/mother/crone or father/son/holy spirit), Ireland

THE ORACLE SAYS: You are being told by the Universe that you are being looked after and to have faith. If a clover, particularly a four-leafed clover, has appeared in your cup, expect good luck in all areas, particularly love and money.

☕ COBWEB

KEY MESSAGES: connectedness, environmental issues, an entanglement

THE ORACLE SAYS: In Native American cultures, Grandmother Spider wove a web that linked us all – the earth, the plants, the animals, humans, even stones and water. The message of the importance of connectedness is being bought to your notice. Are you actively setting an intention for connectedness in your life each day?

ADDITIONAL INSIGHTS: If the cobweb is on the bottom of the cup, this may signify a sticky situation that may be difficult to free yourself from.

☕ COIN

KEY MESSAGES: finance, exchange, profit

THE ORACLE SAYS: Money will be flowing to you certainly, but more abundance will be generated if you learn how to manage money better. You may believe that you are getting a fair exchange for your income but this belief may need to be questioned. Look at your current beliefs around money. Are they all conducive to continual prosperity?

ADDITIONAL INSIGHTS: If a number of coins appear near the handle of the cup, it means that money will be coming soon from multiple sources.

☕ COMB

KEY MESSAGES: attention to detail, vanity/indifference, gossip

THE ORACLE SAYS: You may wish to put a certain situation 'through a fine-toothed comb' before making a decision. Not everything is as it seems. Your physical appearance is being judged…don't be too vain or too indifferent.

☕ COMET

KEY MESSAGES: a quick career trajectory, a hot but short romance, the unexpected

THE ORACLE SAYS: Like a bright comet blazing across the sky once in a decade, all is exciting, hot and bright. Expect the unexpected as nothing will ever be as it was.

☕ COMMA

KEY MESSAGES: a rest or pause, take it slowly

THE ORACLE SAYS: In the whirlwind of the modern world we sometimes forget that fast isn't always best. It is time to take a break and refresh, or at least slow our pace. This will be for our own benefit and will ensure better end results in what ever we are attempting.

☕ COMPASS

KEY MESSAGES: soul purpose, holding an intention, a new direction, travel

THE ORACLE SAYS: Hold on to your true North! If you are in the middle of achieving a long held goal, keep strong to that direction. If it's a new intention and obstacles seem like they keep blocking the way, a new bearing needs to be taken.

ADDITIONAL INSIGHTS: A compass near the rim of the cup means travel is in your very near future.

☕ CONDOM

KEY MESSAGES: protection, putting up a barrier, exercising caution in a sexual relationship

THE ORACLE SAYS: Do you have a pattern of consistently giving too much of yourself in a relationship and forgetting what is important to you? Do you choose sexual partners who take little responsibility for their actions either physically or mentally? The Universe asks that you remember that boundaries are a healthy thing and that losing your Self in a relationship leads to dysfunction.

☕ CORKSCREW

KEY MESSAGES: things are not straight forward, hidden opportunity

THE ORACLE SAYS: Do not expect a project or plan to go easily and in a straightforward manner. There will be plenty of kinks and curves to your progress, however you will get there eventually. The opportunity is still open.

 CORN

KEY MESSAGES: nourishment, wealth

THE ORACLE SAYS: You will be nourished in body, mind and spirit. Feed your appetite for the things that make your heart sing. An increase in your income is highly likely.

 COW

KEY MESSAGES: contentedness, easing of past troubles, thoughtfulness

THE ORACLE SAYS: Cows are symbols of peace and contentedness, so know that there is very little to worry about. Chew over some new ideas as putting some serious consideration to them will allow them to grow and become more useful.

CRAB

KEY MESSAGES: lateral thinking, boundaries, a person who is born under the sign of Cancer from 22nd June to 23rd July.

THE ORACLE SAYS: Don't just go for the obvious solution. This problem will be solved by some lateral and creative thinking. Ensure that you have your personal boundaries intact, as someone may try to get under your defenses.

 CRADLE

KEY MESSAGES: a birth, early development, healing the past

THE ORACLE SAYS: It's time to rejoice – a baby will be born to you or someone close to you or a new idea will be manifested. If a new venture is in its early stages, time and effort should be put in now to ensure its future development.

ADDITIONAL INSIGHTS: A cradle appears on the bottom of the cup indicating that the wounds of the past will or should be healed.

CRANE

KEY MESSAGES: grace, spirituality, a person from Japan, a tall person

THE ORACLE SAYS: The elegant solution, the one that is simple and graceful with the least complexity, is the one you should choose. You are being called upon to discover more about your spiritual side and how it interplays with your day–to–day life.

CUP

KEY MESSAGES: abundance, opportunity, support

THE ORACLE SAYS: Your cup is running over with abundance in love and money! You will continue to be offered great opportunities and will be supported as you ground these in reality.

ADDITIONAL INSIGHTS: If the cup is upside down it may indicate that you will receive a piece of news that is false, but being passed off as fact. Beware of gossip. Place your attention back onto yourself.

CYCLONE

KEY MESSAGES: emotional stress, being buffeted by life

THE ORACLE SAYS: Batten down the hatches – a storm approaches! You may experience a short and intense period of emotional stress but things will get calmer. Try to remain as calm as you can in the eye of the storm…things will pass. A little chaos can be a good thing.

☕ DAGGER (see Knife)

☕ DANCER

KEY MESSAGES: grace, happiness, celebration

THE ORACLE SAYS: There will soon be a reason to dance as a long held wish will be realised or someone close to you will celebrate a personal triumph.

☕ DART

KEY MESSAGES: focus, target

THE ORACLE SAYS: You may well be the focus of a positive intention or the target for some unwelcome attention. Keep your wits about you so that you can tell the difference.

☕ DEVIL

KEY MESSAGES: revolution, uncontrollable lust, a cheeky man

THE ORACLE SAYS: Don't worry unnecessarily about having a visit from the devil in your cup! A devil signifies that things may not keep to the status quo for much longer and someone may well rock the boat. It may be you! Watch out for a man with a cheeky sense of humour or a mischievous smile.

☕ DIAMOND

KEY MESSAGES: commitment, clarity, beauty

THE ORACLE SAYS: Is he or she serious about you? If a diamond appears in your cup it's certain that this person is as committed as it gets! If your question is in regards to a business situation, know that the outcome is clear or has already been decided.

ADDITIONAL INSIGHTS: If the diamond is on the bottom of the cup it's a reminder that your paramour is indeed serious but a marriage proposal is some time off yet.

☕ DISCO BALL

KEY MESSAGES: fun, a party, extroversion

THE ORACLE SAYS: This is no time to be a wallflower. You need to be seen and seen in dynamic action. A party invitation is on its way. Accept it.

☕ DOG

KEY MESSAGES: loyalty, friendship, trust, your dog

THE ORACLE SAYS: A friendship is a true and long lasting one. There has been no betrayal, only a misunderstanding of sorts. You may be called upon to display loyalty to a friend or colleague.

ADDITIONAL INSIGHTS: Sometimes the dog in the cup may refer to your own animal companion. Check to see whether the dog actually looks like or reminds you of your dog. Then, check the other symbols in the cup for clues about what the Oracle may be revealing about him or her.

DOLL

KEY MESSAGES: pretension, falseness

THE ORACLE SAYS: A person who is vain or pretentious is causing agitation in your life. Know that this shallowness comes from a base of fear and self-loathing so this insight may help you deal with them more easily.

DOLPHIN

KEY MESSAGES: freedom, journey over water, overcoming fear

THE ORACLE SAYS: You will experience a profound sense of relief as a fear will be soon overcome. Supported by forces known and unknown, you will then experience a freedom from stresses that have affected you for some time. A journey over water is likely or a destination where you will find yourself in water will be enjoyed within the short-term.

DOVE

KEY MESSAGES: peace, hope, spiritual messages

THE ORACLE SAYS: The symbol of a dove as a spiritual messenger of hope and peace is almost universal. Trust that there will be a respite in the difficulties that are faced and that peace will reign.

ADDITIONAL INSIGHTS: A dove at the bottom of the cup indicates that healing is occuring but not yet completed.

DRAGON

KEY MESSAGES: powerful allies, fierce energy, an attractive newcomer, China

THE ORACLE SAYS: The way to resolve the issue is to place a direct and powerful energy in to it. Now is not the time to just stand there and wait. If your query relates to business, the Oracle advises to reach out and negotiate with those in a more powerful position than you. These people will become useful allies.

DRAGONFLY

KEY MESSAGES: dynamic energy, new opportunities, increase in workload

THE ORACLE SAYS: An imminent burst of new work or opportunities is upon you. You may feel overwhelmed unless you prepare for this. Harmony will be quickly restored if you learn to enjoy the process.

☕ DRUM

KEY MESSAGES: communication, exposure, Africa

THE ORACLE SAYS: Drums in the cup indicate that your message or story will be broadcast to a wide audience. Ensure that the communication is clear and well – crafted so that the message is transmitted successfully. Beware of gossip or miscommunication and leave no room for misunderstandings.

ADDITIONAL INSIGHTS: On the bottom of a cup, a drum foretells scandal and the exposure of news best kept private.

☕ DUCK

KEY MESSAGES: prosperity through hard work, monetary wins, jealousy

THE ORACLE SAYS: Keep an eye out for income from unexpected sources. Generally, your prosperity will grow in direct proportion to your healthy work ethic.

☕ EAGLE

KEY MESSAGES: excellence, bravery, leadership, USA

THE ORACLE SAYS: A true leader can take both a bird's eye view and still see the minutiae of the situation. You are being counseled to develop yourself towards excellence in your field and being the best you can be.

ADDITIONAL INSIGHTS: If the eagle is at the bottom of the cup, it suggests the fall of a mighty leader.

☕ EAR

KEY MESSAGES: listening, secrets

THE ORACLE SAYS: Listening is a highly underrated skill in today's extroverted world, but seeing an ear in your cup encourages you to re-learn this art. It is important to keep your ear to the ground, particularly at work. There may be an opportunity that may only come your way if you hear about it through an unexpected source.

ADDITIONAL INSIGHTS: If the ear is near or at the bottom of the cup, gossip or misinformation may be being spread about you or someone close to you.

☕ EASEL

KEY MESSAGES: creativity, support, an artistic individual, a gallery

THE ORACLE SAYS: Support for all creative undertakings is promised. If you are an artist, this symbol indicates that you should continue to develop your art and that a substantial patron or client is just around the corner. If you are invited to an artistic event or gallery, attend. You may meet someone special there.

 EEL

KEY MESSAGES: masculine energy, slippery, hidden

THE ORACLE SAYS: There are two distinctly different messages should an eel slither into your coffee cup. The first is that masculine energy is needed to solve or resolve a situation. This is a positive interaction. The second message is not so positive. It involves watching out for a 'slippery' individual who cannot be trusted.

 EGG

KEY MESSAGES: fertility, new beginnings, pregnancy

THE ORACLE SAYS: A fresh start is in the offering. New beginnings of all kinds…loves, opportunities, ideas, jobs, health are symbolised by the egg. Should you be trying to conceive a child this is a very positive omen.

 EIGHT

KEY MESSAGES: change, eternity

THE ORACLE SAYS: The number eight indicates that change is certain. If the number appears with symbols of love or marriage it means that the union will be a long and happy one.

ELEPHANT

KEY MESSAGES: lucky, prosperity, wisdom, strength, Africa/Asia

THE ORACLE SAYS: Elephants have always been symbols of great fortune and in particular, sustained prosperity. An elephant in your cup with an upturned trunk is particularly favorable. Before making a key business decision, some thought on the long-term consequences is required.

ELK (Stag)

ENVELOPE

KEY MESSAGES: communication via mail, confidential information

THE ORACLE SAYS: You will receive an official document or notification. Ensure any documents that you have that need to remain confidential are protected so that they remain so.

☕ EXCLAMATION MARK

KEY MESSAGES: surprise, danger, urgency

THE ORACLE SAYS: Pay attention! There is an issue that you need to give your full attention to or alternatively a surprise will soon be unleashed upon you. Consider the other Oracle symbols in your cup for more clarity.

☕ EYE

KEY MESSAGES: clarity, vision, watch carefully

THE ORACLE SAYS: Open your eyes! You are being invited to take a second or third look at something and for good reason – all is not what it seems. If you haven't already done so, creating a vision for your life may clarify some confusion you may have around your personal purpose.

ADDITIONAL INSIGHTS: An eye close to the top of your cup in the 12 o'clock position indicates a need to open your intuition or spiritual outlook more widely.

☕ EYEGLASSES

KEY MESSAGES: clarity, transparency, attention to detail

THE ORACLE SAYS: When we wear eyeglasses we are given a sharper, clearer view. Similarly, this symbol in our cup suggests we look closer and pay special attention to detail.

ADDITIONAL INSIGHTS: If the glass in the eyeglasses looks broken or the symbol is situated very low in the cup, this is a negative omen indicating a restricted or false view is being presented by someone. Don't believe the hype.

☕ FACE

KEY MESSAGES: meaning depends upon expression, resemblance to someone

THE ORACLE SAYS: Does the face resemble someone? If so, this person will play a significant role in your life in the future.
For example
Happy face: positivity, yes, happy outcome
Sad face: negativity, no, sorrow
Winking face: confidence, mischief, everything is okay, lighten up
Profile: someone will be turning away from you or a project, you turning away, ignorance.
Looking right: move forward, new path
Looking left: look for solutions in the past, stay where you are
Looking up: spiritual support, someone with a higher rank, rational thought
Looking down: someone younger or less experienced, emotional thought

ADDITIONAL INSIGHTS: The expression on the face that you are seeing in the cup determines the significance of that face for you in relation to your question.

☕ FAIRY

KEY MESSAGES: whimsy, a garden, romance, a mischievous little girl

THE ORACLE SAYS: So you have a fairy living in your coffee cup rather than your garden? Fairies generally have a light, whimsical and happy disposition and they foretell of romances and relationships that are just as breezy. If you are unattached and seeking a romantic relationship, this omen suggests that you are already attracting that person simply by asking for them. Just ensure you are focused on exactly the kind of person you wish to attract.

FAN

KEY MESSAGES: cooling, flirtation

THE ORACLE SAYS: Whilst it is certainly enjoyable to flirt or be flirted with, expect that nothing more that a little fun will come from this encounter. If the fan is close to the bottom of the cup or is combined with a symbol of money it means that someone will renege on a deal or cool on a business decision.

FANG

KEY MESSAGES: primal reactions, fierceness, intimidation

THE ORACLE SAYS: There may be a situation that makes you so angry or fearful that a certain primal response is triggered in you leaving little time to think through the consequences. Try to stand back and think before you act. Do not be intimidated, your brain here is more powerful than the brawn.

ADDITIONAL INSIGHTS: If the fang is on the bottom of the cup, it indicates a highly charged encounter with the possibility of physical danger.

⚘ FEATHER

KEY MESSAGES: lightness, flight/groundedness, birds, justice

THE ORACLE SAYS: Feathers are generally about intention. Is the person too flighty or light-hearted to stick at the task? Are they taking the situation too lightly? Does the situation call for someone who is more grounded and heavyweight in their knowledge and style?

ADDITIONAL INSIGHTS: If the feather is combined with a cap or hat it means that you have earnt an allocade or that you have learnt something of worth. If the feather is combined with a set of scales, this indicates that justice will be done.

⚘ FEET

KEY MESSAGES: travel, escape, local news, naturalness

THE ORACLE SAYS: A foot or feet in your cup signifies a need to travel to broaden your mind and to relax. It can also indicate a desire to escape from ones current environment. If this is so, escaping is merely part of the answer…things will be the same upon return if steps are not taken to resolve the situation in other constructive ways. Additionally the appearance of a bare foot print can indicate a desire or a suggestion to go back to basics.

☕ FENCE

KEY MESSAGES: boundaries, obstacles

THE ORACLE SAYS: It is a natural, healthy process to have personal boundaries set to protect and nourish you. Do you have these kinds of boundaries? Or is your energy consistently being drained by others? Alternatively, do you overstep the boundaries of others or disrespect their time and energy? It's now time to look at how boundaries help or hinder your life journey at present.

ADDITIONAL INSIGHTS: A fence very low around the cup indicates obstacles that need to be overcome.

☕ FERN

KEY MESSAGES: delicacy, revelations, fertility

THE ORACLE SAYS: Tread carefully; the situation requires the utmost delicacy for it to unfold in the way that you wish. Do not rush things. The fern also indicates male potency.

☕ FERRIS WHEEL

KEY MESSAGES: repetition, awareness of patterns

THE ORACLE SAYS: Feeling deja vu? You have been in this place and situation before and going around again does not serve you well. Break the pattern once and for all.

FIG

KEY MESSAGES: fertility, abundance, satisfaction

THE ORACLE SAYS: Take advantage of the positive omen of the fig and relax knowing that all areas of your life will experience abundance and fertile growth.

FIN

KEY MESSAGES: warning, caution

THE ORACLE SAYS: A fish fin, particularly a shark's fin, present in your cup is warning you about an unseen enemy or that you are playing in waters too deep for you. Get out of the water and reassess the situation.

FISH

KEY MESSAGES: success, fertility, good news from overseas, someone who is a Pisces born 20th February to 20th March

THE ORACLE SAYS: A single fish or a school of fish swimming in your coffee cup heralds a period of great success and good fortune. Fish are also Oracles that women normally receive when they are expressing their creativity to the fullest, especially when they are conceiving children.

ADDITIONAL INSIGHTS: A fish at the bottom of the cup indicates that someone is fishing for information or for an opinion that you are reluctant to give. A fish hook advises caution...you may be caught unawares.

 FIVE

KEY MESSAGES: love, happiness, travel overseas

THE ORACLE SAYS: Spotting a number five in your cup is a lucky omen. It indicates better luck in matters of the heart and in family matters. Also ensure you have your passport ready, as an overseas trip is in your future.

FLOWER

KEY MESSAGES: growth, love, success, recognition

THE ORACLE SAYS: Flowers are always wonderful to receive, especially in your coffee cup! Your life will be blessed with all kinds of growth both materially and spiritually, plus a boost to your love life is also forecasted.

ADDITIONAL INSIGHTS: A bouquet of flowers indicates recognition for a job well done or news of a marriage.

 FLY

KEY MESSAGES: irritation, gossip, illness

THE ORACLE SAYS: We wave flies away as a nuisance and this is what we should do with the little annoyances that are or will be occurring day to day. These are not important so keep your eye on the big picture.

ADDITIONAL INSIGHTS: A fly buzzing at the bottom of the cup indicates an illness or disease.

FOOTBALL

KEY MESSAGES: overlooked, lack of commitment

THE ORACLE SAYS: Footballs are passed and tossed around…just like your opinions or projects will be unless you take action. Consider whether you are too afraid to speak up, or you need to change direction or strategy so that what you offer is more attractive?

FORK

KEY MESSAGES: choice, support, a restaurant

THE ORACLE SAYS: You have a choice to make. There are probably three ways to go. You have the support of others, so do not be afraid to ask for help.

FROG

KEY MESSAGES: growth, female fertility, new love

THE ORACLE SAYS: Both money and love will increase if you have a frog in your cup. If you are single, a frog indicates a new love will find you soon. If you are in a committed relationship, your relationship is destined to grow to a whole new level. Children are also indicated.

FRUIT

KEY MESSAGES: plenty, prosperity, positivity, health

THE ORACLE SAYS: A bunch or bowl of fruit suggests abundance in all things, particularly money. If close to the rim, it indicates good health.

☕ GALLOWS

KEY MESSAGES: failure, self-sabotage

THE ORACLE SAYS: The emphasis here is to know and love your Self more and to be aware that you may be following a set of behaviors that will only sabotage your success. This may be a repeating pattern and one that has cost you dearly in the past.

ADDITIONAL INSIGHTS: A gallows that appears with a person in your cup means that this person will have a hand in a potential failure.

☕ GATE

KEY MESSAGES: allowance, opportunity, entrance

THE ORACLE SAYS: A fantastic opportunity is ready and waiting. The gate is wide open and it is simply enough to walk through to pick up your prize. Don't argue, don't fuss, and don't worry…this time it is easy.

ADDITIONAL INSIGHTS: If the gate looks closed it may mean that you have missed an opportunity.

☕ GENIE

KEY MESSAGES: surprise, wishes granted, a helpful stranger

THE ORACLE SAYS: Rub that coffee cup because seeing a genie appear in it signifies that a long held wish will be granted. Just be careful what you wish for!

☕ GEMINI (astrological symbol is twins)

KEY MESSAGES: someone who is born between 22nd May and 21st June, twins, communication

THE ORACLE SAYS: You can expect clear and considered communication from a Gemini and being understood is of the utmost importance. There is an importance placed on concise decision-making and clear instruction.

☕ GIRAFFE

KEY MESSAGES: view from the top, gentleness

THE ORACLE SAYS: The gentle giraffe asks you to take a higher view. It's amazing how different your opinion may be if you take another look from an alternate angle.

☕ GOAT

KEY MESSAGES: hardiness, determination, dominance, underestimated, a Capricorn – someone born between 22nd December and 20th January

THE ORACLE SAYS: The humble goat is often underestimated. They are tough little animals whose hardiness, versatility and determination put them in good stead in the harshest conditions. By spotting a goat in your cup, you are being reminded that these qualities will be needed in your life.

ADDITIONAL INSIGHTS: A goat at the bottom of your cup indicates a dominant person who may have no ethics about getting to the top. Watch out or you may be butted out of the way.

☕ GRASS

KEY MESSAGES: growth, improvements, home life

THE ORACLE SAYS: Greener pastures are in view for you. Your situation will improve significantly. There will be a renewed emphasis on home and family in the short term. This is a great time to undertake renovations or landscaping for the garden.

☕ GRASSHOPPER

KEY MESSAGES: lack, hunger, greed, poor planning

THE ORACLE SAYS: The grasshopper is traditionally a symbol of famine and the insatiable hunger of the swarm. You are being warned of tougher times due to lack of foresight and preparation.

☕ GRIFFIN

KEY MESSAGES: protection/danger

THE ORACLE SAYS: This mythical beast has a long and interesting history, but normally symbolises the connection between protection and danger. Be warned that the lower the griffin appears in the cup, the more danger is apparent. The danger may or may not be a physical one, but instead it could be someone trying to cheat you or even a poor investment. A griffin high in the cup, particularly at the 12 o'clock position, means that you are protected and you will see the danger coming.

☕ GUITAR

KEY MESSAGES: harmony, thoughtfulness, someone who plays the guitar

THE ORACLE SAYS: A guitar in your cup advises a deeper mindfulness or thoughtfulness about an issue or problem. This will bring resolution and harmony to the situation.

☕ GUN

KEY MESSAGES: trouble, violence, defense/attack

THE ORACLE SAYS: A gun in a coffee cup is not a good omen. Be prepared for some trouble at the very least and there may be the necessity to defend yourself or your family from someone who bears malice towards you.

☕ HAIR

KEY MESSAGES: feral, wild, frightening, risks

THE ORACLE SAYS: Sometimes the patterning in the cup doesn't have a particular image, but it has a very strong texture. If your cup looks 'hairy' it can indicate a return to baser instincts. You may feel a certain wildness or an uncontrollable chaos that can be frightening.

☕ HAMMER

KEY MESSAGES: deliberate intent, physical labour, an intense person

THE ORACLE SAYS: Recognise that it will take some intense focus and perhaps some physical labour to see a project to completion. A person who is highly dedicated or direct may feature in your life in the near future.

☕ HAND

KEY MESSAGES: friendship, assistance, hard work

THE ORACLE SAYS: In the short term, you will receive encouragement and assistance from a close friend. In the longer term, you may need to work with intensity to achieve you goals.

ADDITIONAL INSIGHTS: Shaking hands indicate an agreement will soon be reached on a long-standing issue.

☕ HANDCUFFS

KEY MESSAGES: restriction, legal problems

THE ORACLE SAYS: Your freedom to choose may well be restricted if you continue to follow your current path. Any existing legal problems may become more complex. Be mindful about the law…you may attract more than your fair share of traffic fines!

☕ HANDKERCHIEF

KEY MESSAGES: sorrow, grief, a parting

THE ORACLE SAYS: Seeing a handkerchief in your cup is a sad omen. You may find yourself grieving or experiencing an unexpected parting. Know that this is just a natural part of the cycle of life.

☕ HARE (see Rabbit)

☕ HARP

KEY MESSAGES: angelic assistance, calm, respite

THE ORACLE SAYS: The appearance of this elegant and beautiful instrument foretells a period of relaxation and calm. For those of you who put your faith in angelic guides, this is a confirmation that they are watching and helping.

 HARPY

KEY MESSAGES: warning, story telling

THE ORACLE SAYS: The ancient Greeks believed that flying female entities called Harpies warned sailors of foul weather. It was only later that they got undeserved reputations as wild demons that killed those they sang to. Should a Harpy visit your coffee, there is a warning to heed. Be watchful, be aware and do not take decisions lightly.

HAT

KEY MESSAGES: change, luck, a new home, commitment in love

THE ORACLE SAYS: Expect a change in your job or home if you see a hat in your cup. Chances are you'll be moving to a new address or changing career within six months. A relationship which has been quite open or casual may also become more committed.

HATCHET

KEY MESSAGES: peace, surrender, forgiveness

THE ORACLE SAYS: Whilst it may be a difficult step to take, you are advised to bury the hatchet and seek a peaceful solution. All the better if you can stretch this to include forgiveness.

☕ HAWK

KEY MESSAGES: war, attention

THE ORACLE SAYS: It is time to place all your attention on to something or someone. There may be arguments and debates at work or at home.

☕ HEADSTONE

KEY MESSAGES: remembrance, death, completion, a legacy

THE ORACLE SAYS: Whilst the appearance of a headstone can often mean the death of someone or that you will receive a legacy from a will, it can also indicate a completion.

☕ HEART

KEY MESSAGES: love/heartache, generosity

THE ORACLE SAYS: Yes love is definitely the main subject in your cup, but it can signify different aspects of this emotion. For those looking for love, love is on its way. For those in love already this love will increase…or if other ill omens are present in the cup or the heart looks broken in any way, prepare yourself for heartache. Being forewarned is being forearmed, so you may be able to head a break up off before it happens.

☕ HELICOPTER

KEY MESSAGES: a higher view, looking at the big picture

THE ORACLE SAYS: Imagine how a situation would look from a higher, broader perspective. You are advised not to look at an issue in a shallow way or from too close, or you'll miss the bigger picture.

☕ HELMET

KEY MESSAGES: protection, an intellectual attack, success mentally

THE ORACLE SAYS: Be prepared for some intellectual jousting at the least or a long protracted mental battle at the most. Legal matters often appear this way as do fights over wills or property. Expect great exam results.

☕ HEN

KEY MESSAGES: home, contentment, a 'motherly' type of woman

THE ORACLE SAYS: A hen fussing in your cup indicates a happy time in the home and much to be thankful for. A woman who has mothering energy or is quite home obsessive may enter your life.

⚏ HERON

KEY MESSAGES: psychic abilities, higher reasoning, Japan

THE ORACLE SAYS: The heron is a traditional symbol of spiritual matters and guides us to place importance on the higher reasons for doing things rather than the baser reasons. Think about ethics above need, or honour above dishonesty, for example.

⚏ HILL

KEY MESSAGES: gradual success, obstacles

THE ORACLE SAYS: The bigger or steeper the hill in your cup, the bigger the obstacles in your path. You will succeed, but it will take time and considerable ingenuity.

⚏ HIPPOPOTAMUS

KEY MESSAGES: strong parental love, unexpected strength

THE ORACLE SAYS: There is nothing more ferocious than a hippo blocked from its baby or from its territory. Do not be surprised if you are the recipient of such loyalty and love…or that as a parent, you must display it yourself.

☕ HOLLY

KEY MESSAGES: Christmas, kissing

THE ORACLE SAYS: Holly is an ancient plant of good luck and is a symbol of Christmas cheer. If it appears in your cup, the timing specified will be at Christmas or thereabouts. Also, if it appears alongside omens of love, expect lots of kissing! If Christmas is close when you do the reading, expect an especially happy celebration.

☕ HOOK

KEY MESSAGES: curiosity/addiction, trickery, gullibility, fisherman

THE ORACLE SAYS: In its most positive form, a hook in the cup can indicate a healthy curiosity or a new hobby or even a way of life that will excite you. On the flip side, a hook can also indicate both that some one will 'hook you in' to something that does not serve you, or that an interest turns into an obsession.

☕ HORN

KEY MESSAGES: plenty, positive news, powerful male

THE ORACLE SAYS: A horn is usually a very positive omen. It indicates that there is a plentiful supply of everything that you need materially and that you can expect this to continue for some time. A horn may also indicate good news, often from far away or from a source that you haven't seen in quite a while.

ADDITIONAL INSIGHTS: If the horn is on the bottom of the cup it indicates a powerful male may try to stake his claim or control over your finances.

☕ HORSE

KEY MESSAGES: freedom, power, integrity, healthy self-love, good fortune in love

THE ORACLE SAYS: The mighty horse is something that most of us would like in our cup once in a while. It has many meanings, depending on the visual, but all are generally positive. Horses are extremely powerful animals and increased personal power is signified by seeing one in the cup.

ADDITIONAL INSIGHTS:
Stationary horse: Security, stability and the ability to make wise decisions with intuition.
A running horse: Need for freedom. Travel to the country or a place with open fields.
Horse with rider: Good news from a distance is coming towards you.
Sitting horse: It is more beneficial to stay put than to travel or move. Allow the good fortune to come to you!

Horses head: Your relationship is a deep and connected one. For those who wish for a relationship, you will soon meet a partner who is full of integrity and honesty.

Winged horse: (Pegasus) You are connected with the Divine and you can expect great flow in your life. Everything will move forward with ease and clear direction.

HORSE SHOE

KEY MESSAGES: luck

THE ORACLE SAYS: A horseshoe in your cup is an easy omen to read: it simply means good luck. However, if the horseshoe is turned upside down, luck is running out!

HOUR GLASS

KEY MESSAGES: time, timeliness, decision-making

THE ORACLE SAYS: Are the sands running out for you? Do you feel you have plenty of time or does your intuition tell you that the time for decision-making is now?

HOUSE

KEY MESSAGES: home life, moving/staying, domesticity

THE ORACLE SAYS: All the focus is on your home and home life. You are being urged to pay careful attention to all things domestic. You may be moving house shortly or even purchasing a new home.

☕ HUMMINGBIRD

KEY MESSAGES: delicacy, gathering information, variety

THE ORACLE SAYS: Like feathered butterflies that flit from flower to flower, hummingbirds hover delicately and extract exactly what they want. Similarly, there may be a need to find out information from a variety of sources before making up your mind. Treating a situation with delicacy and care is also urged.

☕ HURDLE

KEY MESSAGES: obstacles, unexpected problems

THE ORACLE SAYS: Yes, having a hurdle or two in your cup seems like a negative thing, however you can still win a race by jumping them. It's very much about attitude and preparedness.

ICE

KEY MESSAGES: cold, frozen, cool rationality

THE ORACLE SAYS: You are being urged to take an emotionless, objective look at an issue. There has been some hot headedness and it is now time to see things very rationally and coolly. Seeing an ice cube in your cup can also indicate frozen emotions. Have you been burying your emotions and keeping them on ice so you don't feel the pain associated with experiencing them?

ICEBERG

KEY MESSAGES: hidden danger, more than meets the eye, secrecy

THE ORACLE SAYS: Most of the mass of an iceberg is hidden from notice under the water, and this is what makes it dangerous. Do not be caught unprepared.

ICE CREAM

KEY MESSAGES: happiness, sweetness, children, summer

THE ORACLE SAYS: There is nothing quite like an ice cream cone on a hot summer's day is there? It's sweet and cool and certainly brings you back to the carefree times you had as a child. Seeing ice cream in your coffee cup invites happiness and innocence back into your life. You have your troubles licked!

♨ ICICLE

KEY MESSAGES: reduction, cooling of ardor or relationship

THE ORACLE SAYS: Although icicles look beautiful, if they appear in your cup you are to be advised that a relationship, agreement or love affair will cool. On the other hand, if the icicle appears with other generally positive symbols, it may mean that obstacles and challenges will slowly reduce, drip by drip.

♨ INITIALS

KEY MESSAGES: a person whose name begins with these initials, or a company name

THE ORACLE SAYS: Identify the initials, and you have identified someone or some entity that will become important in your life very soon.

ADDITIONAL INSIGHTS: If the initials appear on the bottom of the cup, beware. This person or entity may not be a positive influence.

♨ INSECT

KEY MESSAGES: insignificant challenge, anxiousness, small fears

THE ORACLE SAYS: There is nothing to worry about. The fears that you have are not justified.

☕ INVITATION

KEY MESSAGES: receiving an invitation, a challenge

THE ORACLE SAYS: An invitation appearing in your cup is just that. It's inviting you to an event or to step up to a challenge. If the invitation appears with other symbols relating to love, a wedding is soon to occur.

☕ IRON

KEY MESSAGES: reduction of problems, smoothing, pressure

THE ORACLE SAYS: Relax – any troubles or misunderstandings will soon be smoothed over.

ADDITIONAL INSIGHTS: If the iron appears at the bottom of the cup, you will be subjected to increased pressure at work.

☕ ISLAND

KEY MESSAGES: privacy, isolation, solitude, peace, tropical journey

THE ORACLE SAYS: The palm trees are swaying. The azure water is warm and calm. You can see no one, whilst you swing lazily in your hammock. Peaceful isn't it? You have all this to look forward to should an island appear in your cup. You are directed to take some time out from others and concentrate on private pleasures, or at least those with a high degree of sanctuary.

☕ JACK-IN-THE-BOX

KEY MESSAGES: surprise, shock

THE ORACLE SAYS: Whether it's a pleasant surprise or something a little more shocking, seeing a Jack-in-the-box guarantees one thing…you won't see it coming.

☕ JAIL

KEY MESSAGES: trapped, justice, narrow mindedness

THE ORACLE SAYS: Most of us, at one time or another, feel trapped within the life that we lead. Perhaps we see no way out of a situation we find ourselves in. Seeing a jail in your cup indicates that right now that trapped feeling is real for you, however you can change this. The Oracle asks that you open your mind and your heart to changing what currently is, into a life that will bring you more freedom and stimulation.

☕ JAR

KEY MESSAGES: capture, keep, store, create

THE ORACLE SAYS: The slightly old fashioned symbol of a jar is an invitation to keep and store something precious. This is could be something material like money or something not easy to define like a memory. A jar also symbolises long term creativity, so if you are an artist of some kind, this is an auspicious sign.

☕ JELLYFISH

KEY MESSAGES: weakness, directionless, poison

THE ORACLE SAYS: A jellyfish looks quite harmless on the outside, but their sting can be lethal. Is there someone around you who acts in a very innocuous way but your instincts tell you something is not quite right? Is there someone who looks very delicate and doesn't quite commit to any one opinion? It's time to look closer to find the poison that may exist around you.

☕ JEWEL

KEY MESSAGES: wealth, reward, gift, honour

THE ORACLE SAYS: Should you find one or a number of glittering jewels in your coffee cup, expect considerable increase in your money situation or a just reward for your efforts. You may also receive an expensive gift from an unexpected source. For those who are involved in a new love affair, jewels can suggest a valuable jewelry gift will be yours.

☕ JIGSAW PIECE

KEY MESSAGES: clarity, resolution, solutions

THE ORACLE SAYS: At last the puzzle will be solved and you will see the way forward in a totally clear manner. The challenge now will be now to put plans in place to take the best advantage of the situation.

JUDGE

KEY MESSAGES: justice/injustice, legal matters, rules

THE ORACLE SAYS: Know that a situation that requires a fair and just resolution will receive this. Should you be entering into any contracts, play by the letter of the contract.

ADDITIONAL INSIGHTS: If the judge is at the bottom of the cup, this means that justice may not be done if you follow the current strategy.

JUG

KEY MESSAGES: prosperity, plenty, generosity

THE ORACLE SAYS: You will experience a positive flow of prosperity, which may give you so much that your bank account will overflow! Now is the time to be generous with your money, your time and your ideas.

☕ JUGGLER

KEY MESSAGES: variety, feeling overwhelmed, multi-tasking

THE ORACLE SAYS: Whilst most of us in this busy modern world are keen to multi-task, seeing a juggler in your cups warns you that there is too much for you to do. This will only make life too stressful or you will be overwhelmed with confusion and you won't do anything well. Take time to prioritise and to voice that magic word: "NO".

☕ JUMPER

KEY MESSAGES: protection, health issues, winter

THE ORACLE SAYS: You are being warned that your physical body needs protection. Ensure that you are treating it well by eating properly, getting enough sleep and reducing stressors. If you are not feeling up to par, see a professional.

☕ JUNGLE

KEY MESSAGES: confusion, lost, chaos

THE ORACLE SAYS: Yes, it can be a 'jungle out there' and to see one in your cup indicates that you can't see your way out of a situation. You are not lost, it just feels that way. Ask for support from the outside or consult your inner compass, your intuition. The chaos is not real.

☕ KANGAROO

KEY MESSAGES: leaping ahead, balance, high energy, someone from Australia

THE ORACLE SAYS: With perfect poise and balance you will be leaping ahead in all your endeavors. A very positive omen.

☕ KETTLE

KEY MESSAGES: domestic bliss, clarity, visitors to your home

THE ORACLE SAYS: The idea of snuggling up in the comfort of home is bliss for you right now. Home will play a much larger part in your future happiness. Get ready for visitors most likely from overseas or interstate.

☕ KEY

KEY MESSAGES: a solution, a new home, openings

THE ORACLE SAYS: A puzzle will soon be solved and this will pave the way for faster advancement. You may open your heart, your doors, your mind or your eyes to someone or something and this will have major consequences over the short to mid-term.

☕ KITE

KEY MESSAGES: dreams, freedom, aspirations, ambition

THE ORACLE SAYS: You have big dreams and why not! The fulfilment of these dreams will change your life, so ensure that you are up to the challenge by planning and preparing as much as you can.

ADDITIONAL INSIGHTS: If the kite is on the bottom of the cup, it means that plans need more preparation to succeed.

KITTEN

KEY MESSAGES: a gentle young person, innocence, vulnerability/curiosity

THE ORACLE SAYS: Have you ever watched a kitten discovering the world? It's a mixture of startling vulnerability (so tiny, so fragile!) and courage (so curious, so brave!). Perhaps it time to recognise the roles vulnerability and courage play in your life, or of a young person around you. Mentoring may be a great idea.

KNEELING

KEY MESSAGES: reflection, a proposal, begging, humility

THE ORACLE SAYS: If a figure is seen to kneel in your cup you may be called upon to assist someone who is in desperate need and is begging for your help. Alternatively, you may have a problem or issue that seems overwhelming right now and it is being suggested that you take time out to reflect or pray. This should give you more clarity on the matter.

ADDITIONAL INSIGHTS: If the figure kneeling is situated at the bottom of the cup, this suggests the need for humility.

☕ KNIFE

KEY MESSAGES: sharpness, cutting of ties, betrayal

THE ORACLE SAYS: The sharp blade of a knife indicates that there will be a cutting of connection in some way. This may mean a bitter argument, the dissolution of a partnership or even a marriage break up.

ADDITIONAL INSIGHTS: If the knife is opposite the handle of the cup or in the 9 o'clock position, this may mean a betrayal. If the knife is on the bottom of the cup, it means that a plan against you has failed.

☕ KNIGHT

KEY MESSAGES: honour, chivalry, protection

THE ORACLE SAYS: A male who is both honourable and sincere will be entering your life. This person will offer great stability and protection and if you are asking for it, love.

☕ KNITTING

KEY MESSAGES: connection, domestic matters, protection

THE ORACLE SAYS: Knitting was often a way love and protection was shown by the women in the family. Having an image of knitting appear in your cup indicates the need to reconnect with the family or to accept their protection and safety.

KNOT

KEY MESSAGES: obstacles, problems, arguments

THE ORACLE SAYS: Big or small, knots in your cup always signify that the road ahead will not be smooth. It is advisable to look at the situation in its entirety to avoid entanglements.

KOALA

KEY MESSAGES: slow pace, serenity, recovery

THE ORACLE SAYS: A koala in your cup indicates the need to take things far slower than you currently are. The need for serenity and even solitary time apart from others may hasten your desire for healing and wholeness.

KOOKABURRA

KEY MESSAGES: laughter, a comical situation

THE ORACLE SAYS: The appearance of a beautiful laughing kookaburra (kingfisher) indicates that a belly laugh may be on the cards. Be careful though…it could be at your expense!

☕ LACE

KEY MESSAGES: old-fashioned, wedding/christening, patience, success

THE ORACLE SAYS: Seeing a lace pattern amongst your cream is an omen suggesting success though patience or old-fashioned methods. For example, going to see a client face-to-face is going to have more success than sending them an email. For those waiting for a marriage proposal, you may not have to wait for long!

☕ LADDER

KEY MESSAGES: promotion, increases, status

THE ORACLE SAYS: Like in real life, a ladder indicates that you will be stepping up onto a new level. This may mean at work, with money or with education and wisdom. The ascension will be free of challenges.

ADDITIONAL INSIGHTS: If the ladder looks damaged in any way or is lying down it indicates obstacles to your success.

☕ LADLE

KEY MESSAGES: generosity, giving, sharing

THE ORACLE SAYS: You will be the recipient of a valuable piece of advice or a monetary gift. The best results will result from sharing information rather than keeping it to yourself.

☕ LAMP

KEY MESSAGES: enlightenment, discovery, inspiration, leadership

THE ORACLE SAYS: You are being urged to light the way for your Self and for others. It is time to step up into a leadership role and deliberately inspire others towards their goals. Spiritually, you are being called to discover what your true purpose is and how this will affect the world.

ADDITIONAL INSIGHTS: The closer the lamp is to the rim, the more important it is for you to take the leadership position.

☕ LASSO

KEY MESSAGES: off track, incorrect

THE ORACLE SAYS: The strategy you have created is not the way to go. The conclusion that you have made is not accurate. The path you are travelling is taking you further away from your intention. Stop now and reassess.

☕ LEAF

KEY MESSAGES: growth, new starts, new attitude

THE ORACLE SAYS: Welcome a leaf into your cup. It heralds a brand new start and promises healthy growth. You too can turn over a new leaf by ensuring you have learnt from the past.

☕ LEMON

KEY MESSAGES: suspicion, jealousy, sour attitude

THE ORACLE SAYS: Who is it around you that is demonstrating their petty jealousies? Before things get out of hand, it may be worth confronting this person about their misjudged attitude before things sour further.

☕ LION

KEY MESSAGES: bravery, strength, royalty, pride, A Leo – someone born between 24th July and 23rd August.

THE ORACLE SAYS: The mighty lion roars around your cup demonstrating the need for courage and strength in the situation at hand. Do not let pride get in the way of a resolution. Sometimes it is honesty and humble strength that gets you what you want.

☕ LEOPARD

KEY MESSAGES: change/rigidity, control, self-confidence

THE ORACLE SAYS: The old saying that a leopard does not change its spots rings true as an Oracle. You cannot control anyone; it's an illusion of pride that you can. The person who you wish would change needs to decide this for themselves. Free will is an unbreakable Universal Law. You can only suggest what needs to be done. Allow others to live their lives.

☕ LETTER

KEY MESSAGES: news by mail

THE ORACLE SAYS: Expect an important letter in the mail. Should the letter in your cup be surrounded by symbols relating to love, you may receive a heartfelt love letter.

☕ LIBRA (Astrological symbol is the scales)

KEY MESSAGES: gentleness, peaceful, excellence, someone born under the sign of Libra, between 24th September and 23rd October.

THE ORACLE SAYS: There should be no shortcuts to quality or ethics, as a top shelf gift, product or effort is required. The best way to negotiate is the least aggressive. This will achieve the best results for both parties.

☕ LIGHT BULB

KEY MESSAGES: ideas, inspiration, solution

THE ORACLE SAYS: Good news! You will get a fantastic idea which will be a solution to an outstanding problem. If you make your living creatively, this validates that many more good ideas will flow your way.

☕ LIGHTNING

KEY MESSAGES: surprise, unexpected power, energy

THE ORACLE SAYS: Out of the blue, your whole world will change. You may experience a huge epiphany which will change how you think or receive a surprise that enables you to connect with a greater, higher power. Either way, the energy change will be incredible for you.

☕ LINE

KEY MESSAGES: easy/hard, simple/complex

THE ORACLE SAYS: Similar to reading a palm, seeing a line in a cup indicates the qualities of one's life situation now and into the future.

If the line is unbroken and smooth, your path will be an easy one with few complications. If it twists and turns, breaks or shatters, there will be obstacles, hardships and chaos to slow you down.

ADDITIONAL INSIGHTS: The trick here is to ask your questions quite specifically of the Oracle so you get the answer only to that specific question.

♨ LINKS

KEY MESSAGES: connection, weakness/strength, networking

THE ORACLE SAYS: Build rapport and network wisely as your project will be reliant upon the links that you make.

♨ LIPS

KEY MESSAGES: verbal, voice, opinion, gossip

THE ORACLE SAYS: Be acutely aware of what you say about others or what is being said. There is lots of room for verbal misunderstandings. Repeat questions or ask for clarification.

ADDITIONAL INSIGHTS: Should a pair of lips sit at the base of your cup, be mindful of gossip or someone spreading misinformation verbally.

♨ LIPSTICK

KEY MESSAGES: confidence, self-love, a glamorous woman

THE ORACLE SAYS: You are being advised to develop more self confidence and assuredness if you want to achieve your vision and intentions. You are enough, you are perfect, and you know how to succeed. Don't hide your greatness.

☕ LIST

KEY MESSAGES: planning, foresight, memory

THE ORACLE SAYS: You will succeed faster and with fewer hassles if you have a plan. Keep a diary if you don't already.

☕ LIZARD

KEY MESSAGES: overreaction, trust/dishonesty

THE ORACLE SAYS: You may be wondering whether someone around you, or someone that you work with, can be trusted. Whilst they may not act like it, they can be.

ADDITIONAL INSIGHTS: If the lizard rests at the base of your cup, a person around you cannot be trusted.

☕ LOBSTER

KEY MESSAGES: luxury, pleasure, indulgence

THE ORACLE SAYS: A lucky lobster in your cup indicates all things luxe. You may be treated to an expensive outing, an over-the-top gift or an indulgent day out. But why wait for someone else to give it to you? Don't you deserve to treat yourself once in a while?

 LOCK

KEY MESSAGES: security, trapped, secrecy

THE ORACLE SAYS: Be mindful of what needs to remain safe and private and what can be shared. Do not, for one minute, allow for someone you do not completely trust to have access to information that you wouldn't like to be public knowledge. If you are traveling, ensure your house is secure and that your luggage has a lock.

 LOG

KEY MESSAGES: death, laziness, building

THE ORACLE SAYS: A single log is an omen indicating a lazy or boring person or that you have little initiative right now. It may also mean the death of an idea or a project. If there are multiple logs stacked closely. It shows there will be some building occurring. This could be the building of a house, business or idea.

LOOP

KEY MESSAGES: lessons, patterns

THE ORACLE SAYS: Do you keep making the same mistakes over and over? Identify and expose the patterns that no longer serve you. It is now time to learn your lesson so that these negative loops disappear once and for all. They have cost you too much time, money and peace.

LOTUS

KEY MESSAGES: beauty, triumph over adversity, something from nothing

THE ORACLE SAYS: The lotus is one of the world's most beautiful and impressive flowers. Did you know that it grows from the most putrid mud, struggles through dirty water to finally surface to find the sunshine to blossom magnificently? No matter how bad things look, no matter how muddy things get, know that you will succeed. You will not just survive, you will flourish.

LYRE

KEY MESSAGES: happiness, music, thoughtfulness, joy

THE ORACLE SAYS: True joy will drift into your life, just like the softness of the lyre's music. You are also being invited to be more thoughtful about your life and the direction it is going. Mindfulness will only bring greater happiness.

☕ MAGICIAN

KEY MESSAGES: transformation, change, inner wisdom

THE ORACLE SAYS: The magic of transformation is cast over you. It's time to delve deep and decide what changes you want to make in your life, as the time is right.

☕ MAGNET

KEY MESSAGES: attraction

THE ORACLE SAYS: A magnet in your cup indicates a strong attracting force. You may attract money, people and even good luck. Check what other symbols are present in the cup for more information.

☕ MAGPIE

KEY MESSAGES: discovery, lost/found, friendship

THE ORACLE SAYS: You are being asked to exercise an attitude of curiosity – after all, no one knows everything! A solution to a problem may be found by an unexpected discovery. A new friend will soon fly into your life.

☕ MAN (see Person)

 MAP

KEY MESSAGES: journey, travel, destination, treasure

THE ORACLE SAYS: Do you know where you are headed? Do you have a clear destination in mind? If not, finding a map in your cup tells you that the way forward will be made clear and directions will be given to you. You may also be taking a trip or lengthy journey in the near future.

MAPLE LEAF

KEY MESSAGES: improved fortune, Canada

THE ORACLE SAYS: If you haven't been experiencing good luck lately this will now change since a maple leaf has appeared in your coffee.

MARK

KEY MESSAGES: spoil, tarnish, reduce

THE ORACLE SAYS: A mark which covers or changes a particularly clear symbol normally indicates something may attempt to spoil or damage this thing. For example, a mark over a dollar sign may indicate that income coming to you may be delayed or decreased.

🍵 MASK

KEY MESSAGES: false, secrecy, inauthentic

THE ORACLE SAYS: Everyone at some time or another has felt as though they need to hide who they are or wishes to be someone else. However, if a mask appears in your cup, a person of significance in your life is displaying a false front and they are not at all what they present, and this will affect you if not recognised.

🍵 MAT

KEY MESSAGES: dominance, self-esteem, boundaries

THE ORACLE SAYS: Stop acting like a doormat. People will continue to treat you exactly as you allow it. It's time to stop acting the victim and put in place some healthy boundaries that will protect you and give you some self-respect.

🍵 MEDUSA

KEY MESSAGES: troubles in love, a desperate woman

THE ORACLE SAYS: You may feel entangled and frustrated in a difficult romantic relationship. Simplify your communication. Ask questions of your lover to be clear on his or her intention before you react. Watch out for a female intent on achieving her goals. She has few ethics and will stop at nothing.

☕ MEERKAT

KEY MESSAGES: family, protection, matriarchal line

THE ORACLE SAYS: Yes, meerkats may look very cute but they are brave and savage fighters when called upon to protect their family and friends. You may be called upon to stand up for someone close to you. Good news will come from the female side of the family.

☕ MERMAID

KEY MESSAGES: love, a temptation, lust

THE ORACLE SAYS: Should you find a mermaid swimming in your cup chances are you will find someone very attractive who loves the sea or has a job associated with the ocean. They will offer you a lustful temptation!

ADDITIONAL INSIGHTS: Should the mermaid be at the bottom of your cup, the lover who tempts you is not exactly what they seem. You may be out of your depth.

☕ MILK

KEY MESSAGES: nourishment, parental support

THE ORACLE SAYS: Milk is expressed visually by a milk carton, bottle or by your intuition telling you that a glass symbol is filled with milk. It indicates that it's time for you to nourish yourself in body and in mind. Think about how you can actively do this and do it promptly. Milk also indicates that a parent or grandparent will assist you if you ask the right way.

MIRROR

KEY MESSAGES: self examination, self love, beauty

THE ORACLE SAYS: Why is it that you do not love yourself as you should? Perhaps you have issues around your self-image, your body or your age? Spirit reminds you that you indeed are beautiful and are made perfectly to fulfill your sacred purpose in life. Seek further help to heal any body image issues.

MISTLETOE

KEY MESSAGES: Christmas, love, secret love, a gift

THE ORACLE SAYS: If mistletoe is spotted in your cup within three months prior to Christmas, know that something important in regards to your love relationship will happen around this time. If outside this time, expect a surprise gift from an admirer.

MITTEN

KEY MESSAGES: warmth, protection, winter

THE ORACLE SAYS: A business or love relationship that has cooled will soon be warmed up once again.

☕ MONEY

KEY MESSAGES: financial gain

THE ORACLE SAYS: Get ready to watch the balance of your bank account swell, as money is on the way!

☕ MONKEY

KEY MESSAGES: intelligence, playfulness, resourcefulness, mischief

THE ORACLE SAYS: A very intelligent, yet playful person will be entering your life and assisting you in a significant way to achieve a project. You may not trust them at first as their joyful demeanor is misconstrued as frivolous, but nothing could be further from the truth.

ADDITIONAL INSIGHTS: A monkey at the bottom of the cup indicates that someone may be creating mischief to stop you achieving a goal. This may manifest in the form of a joke gone wrong or gossip.

☕ MONGOOSE

Key Messages: courage against the odds, bravery

The Oracle Says: You have a formidable opponent, but know that you can and will win. Your enemy, whether it is a person or a problem, looks huge and fierce, but you are more than ready to face them and to overcome anything they throw at you. Feel brave and confident.

☕ MONSTER

Key Messages: fear of the known and the unknown

The Oracle Says: Our fears get in the way of many things that we feel we want to do. Some of these are healthy fears and some not. The time has come to identify and face your fears. These are the first two steps in heading into the life that you are meant to live. Slay that monster!

☕ MOON

Key Messages: female strengths, love, transformation, cycles

The Oracle Says: The moon is one of the most universal symbols of change in our world. Should Mother Moon appear in your cup, know that transformation is occurring and that things are moving in the direction that you wish. Do not fight the natural cycle of things.

ADDITIONAL INSIGHTS:

Different phases indicate different omens

Crescent moon: new beginnings, a birth, hope.

Half moon: You are half way through a project, progression, connection.

Full moon: positive omen, 'yes', full power, fertility, good timing.

Dark moon: thinking, introversion, making a decision by yourself, boundaries.

Moon with clouds: some obstacles or some barriers will present themselves but you will shine through.

☕ MOOSE/ANTLERS

KEY MESSAGES: male power, protection, integrity

THE ORACLE SAYS: There may be a temptation to lower your ideas and principals for seemingly great reward. Resist the temptation.

☕ MOTH

KEY MESSAGES: magic, night time, message from a stranger or a secret admirer

THE ORACLE SAYS: Although many people would prefer a butterfly, a moth in your cup is normally a good omen. There is magic afoot and the Universe is sending you what you need in a very subtle way. Do not look in the obvious places for a solution.

☕ MOTORBIKE

KEY MESSAGES: speed, agility, danger/freedom

THE ORACLE SAYS: You will get where you want to go faster than you think. Resilience and versatility will be important elements in your strategy.

ADDITIONAL INSIGHTS: If the motorbike is on the bottom of the cup, take extra care on the roads or with a risky activity.

☕ MOUNTAIN

KEY MESSAGES: climbing upwards, a journey

THE ORACLE SAYS: The things that you want right now are going to take time and effort. You need a plan and resources to achieve them, but achieve them you will, slowly but surely. The view from the top is amazing!

☕ MOUSE

KEY MESSAGES: lack, distrust, trap

THE ORACLE SAYS: If a mouse if found in your cup, this normally signals a decrease in income or lack in the finance area. If the mouse appears with other omens indicating money then this is especially so. You may also feel as though you distrust someone in particular at present. Ensure that you undertake sufficient research on this person or their company.

☕ MUMMY

KEY MESSAGES: eternity, faith, death, preservation, Egypt

THE ORACLE SAYS: Spiritually you are being asked questions in regards to your faith. What do you believe in? Nothing? Everything? Walk your walk, don't just talk your talk. There is nothing to be afraid of. Your real Self is always there to come back to.

ADDITIONAL INSIGHTS: A mummy at the bottom of your cup can indicate a physical death, and you are encouraged to see this as a transition for this person. Death is a natural part of the cycle of life.

☕ MUSHROOM

KEY MESSAGES: growth, preparedness, imagination

THE ORACLE SAYS: Have you ever walked through a forest after rain? Often there is a plethora of mushrooms that have seemingly appeared, fully formed, overnight. Seeing a mushroom in your coffee signals rapid growth for those who are prepared. For those of you who are artists of any type, get ready for a wild creative spurt that will lead to more recognition.

🍵 MUSIC

KEY MESSAGES: happiness, harmony, good luck, celebration, a musician

THE ORACLE SAYS: Seeing a single musical note or a veritable symphony in your cup indicates something to sing about. Happiness and increased good fortune are yours.

NAIL

KEY MESSAGES: toughness, resilience, security

THE ORACLE SAYS: A degree of toughness needs to be displayed to forge success in a difficult endeavor. A firmer attitude should not be feared and people will respond favourably to the shift.

NECKLACE

KEY MESSAGES: hereditary gift, family support

THE ORACLE SAYS: You may receive a gift or something of value from a family member. This may be through a formal bequest or simply through an unexpected gift.

NECKTIE

KEY MESSAGES: restrictions, prohibition

THE ORACLE SAYS: Just like when a necktie is done up too tightly, you may be feeling restricted and uncomfortable in your current situation. It's time to be you and loosen up a little. If the situation at hand isn't allowing that, move on. It's just not worth the energy.

☕ NEEDLE

KEY MESSAGES: building, fame, recognition

THE ORACLE SAYS: Get ready to be a whole lot more noticeable. You will be gaining notoriety or at least some recognition for an activity you are doing. If you are the organiser of an event, it will go off without a hitch.

☕ NEST

KEY MESSAGES: security, parenting, protection, building

THE ORACLE SAYS: A nest is built by many small and sometimes insignificant pieces woven together to make something strong yet gentle. You have built a secure sanctuary or set of boundaries over time and rewards will now flow from this. Snuggle up and know that you are protected and safe. This will be a brilliant platform to take off from.

☕ NET

KEY MESSAGES: trapped, patience, connection, organisation

THE ORACLE SAYS: Your organisation skills will be at their sharpest. You will have the power to bring together a disparate group of people with your incisive strategies.

ADDITIONAL INSIGHTS: If the net is placed over the bottom of your cup, you may feel trapped in a situation that was not of your making.

☕ NEWSPAPER

KEY MESSAGES: gossip, news, gathering information

THE ORACLE SAYS: If a newspaper opens in your cup, be prepared for big news with headlines that certainly will affect you in a profound way. Also be aware that there may be plenty of gossip floating about and it is about you. Find out who the instigator is and confront them. Gossips hate being found out…it takes the fun out of it for them!

☕ NIL (zero)

KEY MESSAGES: nothing, no, blank slate

THE ORACLE SAYS: There is nothing to fear or you may receive nothing in a monetary settlement. A nil or zero also indicates a new beginning or blank slate enabling you to rethink and stage another more successful attempt. If you are asking a specific question requiring a positive or negative answer, seeing an O indicates a 'no'.

☕ NINE

KEY MESSAGES: spirituality, higher good, money, travel

THE ORACLE SAYS: Seeing the number nine in your cup is a happy omen and one that often connects you with your higher Self. You may also expect more money in your purse or that you will have the opportunity to travel to somewhere that has a more spiritual bent.

 NOSE

KEY MESSAGES: ignorance, greed, dishonesty

THE ORACLE SAYS: What is it that is going on 'under your nose' but that you cannot see? Stop pleading ignorance! The answer is as close as the nose on your face. A nose may also indicate that a decision may be made with greed as a primary motivator. Use this information to your advantage.

NUN

KEY MESSAGES: chastity, piety, isolation

THE ORACLE SAYS: You are being strongly advised that a more chaste response to a lover is the way to either win his heart or to see his true colours. You may feel lonely and a little isolated, but it is better to see clearly than to be clouded by lust.

NURSE

KEY MESSAGES: care, sickness, medicine

THE ORACLE SAYS: You or someone close to you may experience an illness that needs to be treated. Alternatively you may find yourself acting as a carer for someone who is sick.

 NUT

KEY MESSAGES: prosperity, growth, off balance

THE ORACLE SAYS: Seeing a nut, whether it is a Brazil, cashew or peanut, heralds a time of growth, particularly in the financial sphere. If you can, invest any extra income now and watch it grow.

ADDITIONAL INSIGHTS: If the nut appears on the bottom or by the handle, be wary of an unbalanced or over anxious person. Their judgment is not sound.

OAK

KEY MESSAGES: stability, strength, greatness from humble beginnings

THE ORACLE SAYS: The mighty oak has appeared in your cup signaling that there is stability and endurance in most aspects of your life. Your business, partnership or marriage will continue to be stable and grow from strength to strength.

OAR

KEY MESSAGES: guidance, control, teamwork

THE ORACLE SAYS: You are being asked to take control of your own ship and make your own way under your own steam. Do not be afraid of this, you are being guided. If you do need to get a team involved, ensure that it is you who will be leading the effort.

OCEAN

KEY MESSAGES: prosperity, vastness, power, possibility

THE ORACLE SAYS: Your ability to create prosperity for yourself is as infinite as the ocean. There are no limits to the possibilities open to you at this moment. You possess the power to manifest your purpose even if you at times doubt this. You may also decide to take a rejuvenating break by the sea.

ADDITIONAL INSIGHTS: There is a saying, "Never turn your back on the ocean." This is especially relevant should you see the ocean at the bottom of your cup. There may well be an unexpected danger or a constriction of choice and possibility.

☕ OCTOPUS

KEY MESSAGES: many activities at once, unwelcome interference

THE ORACLE SAYS: Does someone have their tentacles in your affairs? Remove them. Do you feel overwhelmed that you have too many different things going on? Simplify.

☕ ONE

KEY MESSAGES: back to basics, priorities, first, new

THE ORACLE SAYS: Sometimes, we forget about what is important to us in life, and a number one appearing in our cup reminds us about our true priorities. Get ready for a win or a new idea that, although simple, may lead to a happier lifestyle.

ADDITIONAL INSIGHTS: If there are other symbols in the cup relating to romance or relationships, it indicates a new relationship or a fresh start to an existing one.

☕ ONION

KEY MESSAGES: complexity, secrecy, sorrow

THE ORACLE SAYS: Be mindful that a situation or person has many layers. What you are seeing may well be just a fraction of what exists. Do not make your decisions based on limited information.

ADDITIONAL INSIGHTS: If the onion is at the bottom of the cup it is a sign of tears and sorrow. Be mindful here of what other symbols are present in the cup for hints in what area the sorrow may be referred to.

☕ ORANGE

KEY MESSAGES: good health, brighter outlook, restoration

THE ORACLE SAYS: Oranges are happy messengers of radiant health and wellbeing. If you have been feeling down and depressed lately, an orange signifies that this will soon pass.

☕ ORCHID

KEY MESSAGES: exotic, sexual, pressure to perform, Thailand

THE ORACLE SAYS: Orchids are often produced in a hothouse environment. Lots of heat and pressure create their exotic yet delicate beauty. This could indicate a torrid sexual affair or you may be attracted to someone through a high pressure situation, like through business. Be warned though; take the orchid out of the hothouse and it usually withers and dies.

OSTRICH

KEY MESSAGES: ignorance, honesty, fear

THE ORACLE SAYS: Be mindful that you do not have 'your head in the sand' over an important issue. There is no room right now for self-imposed ignorance or fearfulness. Courage and clear thinking is called for.

OTTER

KEY MESSAGES: creativity, building, mischief

THE ORACLE SAYS: Otters are the builders of the animal kingdom, so if one appears in your cup it signifies you will be creating something of substance. They are also cheeky and mischievous creatures so do not be afraid to let go and play a little in your spare time.

OWL

KEY MESSAGES: wisdom, feminine wisdom, spirit world, Athens

THE ORACLE SAYS: Closely linked with the realm of the spirits, owls bring not only the wisdom of this world, but that of others. Taking this into consideration, know that you are being assisted from all sides: from spirit, from your ancestors and from your own wise Self. Listen closely to a woman you consider wise... her advice is sound.

OX

KEY MESSAGES: endurance, hard work, strength, someone who is a Taurean (see Taurus) born between 21st April and 21st May

THE ORACLE SAYS: You are being called upon to demonstrate strength and endurance. You CAN do what you have set out bravely to do.

OYSTER

KEY MESSAGES: secret love, friendship that turns into love, sex

THE ORACLE SAYS: Is there someone who you secretly admire? Or is there a wonderful friendship that could, would or should develop into something more? Your cup indicates that there is a good chance that things may be developing in a more romantic way in the future.

ADDITIONAL INSIGHTS: If the oyster has a pearl in it, it signifies that a long–held wish will come true or that something that started off as an irritation has grown into something far more valuable.

An oyster on the bottom of the cup indicates that greater secrecy is required in a love affair. The less people that know, the better.

☕ PAGODA

KEY MESSAGES: steady progress spiritually, China, Japan

THE ORACLE SAYS: The stepped shape of the pagoda indicates that spiritual progress is being made. Great changes are afoot.

☕ PAINT TUBE

KEY MESSAGES: choice, expression, emotions

THE ORACLE SAYS: There is an almost infinite variety of colours and even shades between black and white. You do have a choice and you have a right to feel the full rainbow of emotions if you so wish. A full expression of ideas or opinions is necessary.

ADDITIONAL INSIGHTS: A paint tube at the bottom of the cup can indicate a creative obstacle like writer's or artist's block.

☕ PAINT BRUSH

KEY MESSAGES: adding colour and variety, change

THE ORACLE SAYS: Spruce up your car, your home or even yourself. A different look can be energising. Change is good.

☕ PALACE (see Castle)

☕ PALM TREE

KEY MESSAGES: tropical, holiday in a tropical place, hidden strength

THE ORACLE SAYS: Have you ever seen the roots of a palm tree? These long and lean trees have huge root balls giving them incredible stability, allowing the trunks effortless flexibility. You too have this hidden strength, now is the time to call upon it.

☕ PAN

KEY MESSAGES: playfulness, decadence, music

THE ORACLE SAYS: The presence of the mythological figure Pan playfully signifies a time of celebration, music and dancing. It may also be a warning to curb too many wild nights and overindulgences such as overeating, drugs and alcohol.

☕ PANTHER

KEY MESSAGES: power, secrecy, South America

THE ORACLE SAYS: This elusive and beautiful creature has always held great power for the indigenous people that it shares its territory with. A panther in your cup can either be interpreted that great power will be invested in you or that there may be someone of great power in the shadows watching your progress.

ADDITIONAL INSIGHTS: A panther prowling at the bottom of your cup indicates a person who may be secretly seeking to lie or trick you. Beware.

☕ PAPER

KEY MESSAGES: recording ideas or issues, journaling, communication via letter

THE ORACLE SAYS: It is time to get your inspiring ideas or dark troubles out of your head and onto paper. This will decrease your stress levels substantially. Although you may feel the art of letter writing is somewhat of date, please reconsider. A short note scripted by your own hand will be greatly appreciated.

☕ PARACHUTE

KEY MESSAGES: a successful landing, leaping forward, trust, courage

THE ORACLE SAYS: You have been courageous enough to leap magnificently forward, you have been protected and will be successful. For those a little less brave, you are encouraged to make your leap after some planning and preparation. You will land safely and gently!

ADDITIONAL INSIGHTS: A parachute at the bottom of the cup signifies the need to have more faith. Trust your Self and others.

☕ PARCEL

KEY MESSAGES: a surprise, a gift, a completion

THE ORACLE SAYS: Here it is, ready, presented to you neatly wrapped up and tied with string. It is complete and you have earnt it. What 'it' is though, only you know!

☕ PARROT

KEY MESSAGES: repetition, someone who gossips or talks too much, travel to a tropical locale

THE ORACLE SAYS: If you keep doing what you are doing, you will keep getting what you are getting. Identify the behavioral patterns that no longer serve you and take steps to avoid them.

☕ PAW

KEY MESSAGES: connection with animals, the wild Self, adventure

THE ORACLE SAYS: As modern humans, most of us compromise on our innate wildness and we tame our Selves so we can operate in ten-storey buildings and concrete jungles.

For our own health and wholeness we need to understand that we too are animals and need the 'wilderness' to refresh and renew. Ideally, take some time out from the city and be amongst nature. At the very least, walk your dog or play wildly with your cat today.

 PAWN

KEY MESSAGES: manipulation, deception, game playing

THE ORACLE SAYS: A pawn suggests that you could be or may already be part of a manipulative game that someone is staging. Be very aware of the motives of the people around you.

 PEA

KEY MESSAGES: small but powerful, hidden issue, a conception

THE ORACLE SAYS: Like the fable of the princess and the pea, something small but significant is bothering you right now. No matter how much you try to forget it, this issue still nags at you. It's time to uncover it and challenge it.

ADDITIONAL INSIGHTS: A pea near the rim of the cup indicates an announcement of a pregnancy.

☕ PEACE SIGN

KEY MESSAGES: peace, ceasing of hostilities

THE ORACLE SAYS: A long held feud will come to an end. This may be quite a sudden and unexpected occurrence.

☕ PEACH

KEY MESSAGES: lust, passion, ripeness, wholeness

THE ORACLE SAYS: Lucky you! A luscious peach in your cup indicates a juicy, lustful encounter is heading your way. You will be the centre of a delicious passion.

☕ PEACOCK

KEY MESSAGES: money, ethical behavior, an attractive male, ego

THE ORACLE SAYS: A peacock shimmering his tail feathers in your coffee heralds great prosperity and the possibility of the partnership with an attractive male. This partnership, whether it is romantic or otherwise, is one characterised by depth and integrity.

ADDITIONAL INSIGHTS: A peacock on the bottom of your cup prompts you to curb your ego and practice some humility.

☕ PEAR

KEY MESSAGES: fertility, new beginnings, a generous woman

THE ORACLE SAYS: You are ripe for a generous proportion of love and lust. Relax and accept this treat as there is no need to be afraid. A woman with an open and generous demeanor may offer you a lucrative opportunity.

☕ PEARL

KEY MESSAGES: growth, beauty, lessons learnt

THE ORACLE SAYS: A pearl has its birth as a small grain of sand or piece of grit inside an oyster. Uncomfortable with this foreign object, the mother of pearl is smoothly placed over it, layer upon layer, transforming this irritant into something of beauty and of value. What has happened in your life that was less than ideal yet has been a great lesson for you? What can you make into your pearl?

☕ PEN

KEY MESSAGES: writing, contracts, a story needing to be recorded

THE ORACLE SAYS: Why are you holding yourself back, dear writer? You are being called to express your Self through the pen. Do not edit what you write and do not judge…just write. Writing this way can be seen as a spiritual practice.

ADDITIONAL INSIGHTS: A pen at the bottom of a cup signifies that a contract or agreement should be signed in a timely manner.

☕ PENDULUM

KEY MESSAGES: balance, forgiveness, indecision

THE ORACLE SAYS: A pendulum appearing in your cup gives you a strong message to make a firm decision on an issue and no longer procrastinate. By making this decision, balance will be restored and movement will return to your life.

ADDITIONAL INSIGHTS: A pendulum at the bottom of the cup is inviting you to forgive a trespass against you.

☕ PENGUIN

KEY MESSAGES: unexpected competence, lighter approach

THE ORACLE SAYS: Whilst the funny little penguin looks awkward as he waddles comically across the ice, he is the polar opposite in his true home, the water. Streamlined and athletic, he cuts through the water at lightning speed catching his prey. Watch out for a similar talent in another person or even yourself. Do not judge a book by its cover!

☕ PENIS

KEY MESSAGES: male power, lust, desire, potency

THE ORACLE SAYS: For female readers: There is certainly someone who has a carnal desire for you. The bigger the penis appears, the stronger the desire! For male readers: There also may be another male who wishes to engage you in a power struggle and reduce your effectiveness, particularly in the workplace. If you are a gay man, there is a man who has a carnal desire for you.

ADDITIONAL INSIGHTS: A penis appearing at the bottom of the cup indicates a lack of potency or effectiveness for both male and females.

☕ PENTAGON

KEY MESSAGES: balance, precision, someone from government

THE ORACLE SAYS: To achieve your vision you must pay attention to detail and not just take a wide view. A pentagon can also signify a balanced situation.

ADDITIONAL INSIGHTS: A pentagon at the bottom of the cup indicates corruption.

☕ PERISCOPE

KEY MESSAGES: investigation, spying

THE ORACLE SAYS: You are being watched from unexpected quarters or you feel the need to secretly investigate something or someone.

☕ PERSON

THE ORACLE SAYS: Seeing a person in your cup can mean a variety of things depending upon what the person 'looks like' and what they are doing. If the person resembles someone you know, this person will feature strongly in your life in the near future. If the person is performing an action, the omen will be different.

Running clockwise: This person is coming towards you to assist or to join you. Running anticlockwise: This person is leaving your life or escaping from something.
Lying Down: This person has given up the struggle or the way of life they have chosen to lead now. This is not necessarily a bad thing. If this figure is on the bottom of the cup it can indicate illness or depression.
Kneeling (see Kneeling)
Pregnant (see Pregnancy)

ADDITIONAL INSIGHTS: Look carefully as this may well be someone you recognize handing you a message. Take note of the other symbols in the cup for a clearer indication of what this person brings you.

☕ PHEASANT

KEY MESSAGES: royalty, hidden beauty, honour

THE ORACLE SAYS: You have a choice, and it's best to do the most honorable thing. Step above the squabbling and the babble and take the higher path.

☕ PHOENIX

KEY MESSAGES: triumph over adversity, rebirth, healing

THE ORACLE SAYS: Seeing the phoenix is a powerful Oracle of renewal. From the ashes of a defeat or dire adversity, rises success and triumph. This is a positive symbol of great healing.

☕ PHONE

KEY MESSAGES: important communication by phone, making a call

THE ORACLE SAYS: You will make or receive a significant phone call which will have important consequences. Alternatively, is there someone who you haven't recently contacted who would appreciate a phone call?

ADDITIONAL INSIGHTS: A phone at the bottom of the cup indicates the likelihood of bad news via a call.

☕ PIANO

KEY MESSAGES: success, musicality, someone musical

THE ORACLE SAYS: Music is one of the creative joys of life, so do partake whether it's listening, playing or creating. Someone highly musical will be entering your life.

☕ PIE

KEY MESSAGES: satisfaction, successful project, greed

THE ORACLE SAYS: Yes, you can have your pie and eat it! A plan will be successful and many people will share in your success.

ADDITIONAL INSIGHTS: A pie at the bottom of your cup may signify greed.

☕ PIG

KEY MESSAGES: prosperity/self-indulgence, joy

THE ORACLE SAYS: There is a fine line between enjoying life and engaging in self-indulgent behavior. In all ways we are worth spoiling, but when we consume too much food or wine, expect too many of the finer things in life or demand things in disrespectful ways, we lose track of what really does give us joy.

ADDITIONAL INSIGHTS: Should you see a pig with tusks such as a boar, this signifies an aggressive male or a male with great influence who may not use his power ethically.

PIGEON

KEY MESSAGES: communication from overseas, returning home

THE ORACLE SAYS: Do you know where your home is? Are you aware of where your place of centering is? If so, you are being called back there or to stay well protected and nourished within its boundaries. If not, perhaps it's time to find your true home both inside and out.

PILLAR

KEY MESSAGES: strength, resilience, protection

THE ORACLE SAYS: There is nothing being presented that you are not strong enough to handle. Your resilience is one of your finest attributes and you will flourish.

ADDITIONAL INSIGHTS: Should the pillar be broken or lying on its side, this means that the protection you have enjoyed has been withdrawn.

PILLOW

KEY MESSAGES: rest, dreams, 'pillow talk'

THE ORACLE SAYS: Body and mind need to be rested if you are to fully appreciate life. Look to your dreams for inspiration and solutions to challenges.

ADDITIONAL INSIGHTS: If the pillow is at the bottom of the cup beware of 'pillow talk'... someone may be spreading gossip or gaining information through the bedroom or through someone who is related to them.

♨ PIN

KEY MESSAGES: rapid change, a dynamic person

THE ORACLE SAYS: The appearance of a pin heralds great change in your life usually around your career or your ambitions. Do not be wary of this, as the changes will be positive as long as you know what you want as an outcome.

ADDITIONAL INSIGHTS: A pin on the bottom of the cup may mean a long held desire disappears.

♨ PINE TREE

KEY MESSAGES: good health, improved health, Christmas

THE ORACLE SAYS: The slightly medicinal smell of pine needles gives a hint to the meaning of this Oracle. You will experience good health and vitality into the future. Something significant will occur around Christmas time.

☕ PINEAPPLE

KEY MESSAGES: a situation that looks hopeless but is not, a tropical destination

THE ORACLE SAYS: A pineapple is fairly uninviting on the outside but sweet and delicious on the inside. Similarly, a situation or event that you have been dreading turns out to be actually quite easy or pleasant.

☕ PIPE

KEY MESSAGES: thoughtfulness, reconciliation, an older man

THE ORACLE SAYS: Combined with a peace symbol or other signs relating to forgiveness, a pipe can mean an end to a long lasting feud or a heartfelt reconciliation. A pipe also encourages some deep introspective thinking or meditation. Both will quiet the mind, reduce inner chatter and result in less stress and unnecessary anxiety.

☕ PIRANHA

KEY MESSAGES: loss, decline

THE ORACLE SAYS: Bit by bit, bite by bite, you are losing something dear to you. This may be a person, a possession, a position or even your own true Self. Stop the decline before it is too late.

☕ PIRATE

KEY MESSAGES: revolution, stealing, adventure

THE ORACLE SAYS: If a swashbuckling pirate appears in your cup he is daring you to break with convention and take more exciting route towards adventure. Try new methods, processes and behaviors and start your own revolution!

ADDITIONAL INSIGHTS: A pirate at the bottom of your cup indicates that you may be the victim of theft of some kind.

☕ PISCES (astrological symbol is two fish)

KEY MESSAGES: someone born between February 20th and March 20th, a dreamer

THE ORACLE SAYS: The symbol of Pisces indicates a gentle soul prone to dreaming and visions.

☕ PISTOL

KEY MESSAGES: defense/attack, war, trouble

THE ORACLE SAYS: You may find yourself on the defense or alternatively attacking, to protect a principal, a person or even yourself. This is a strong omen and all care should be taken to avoid physical harm.

♨ PITCHFORK

KEY MESSAGES: anger, hatred, resentment

THE ORACLE SAYS: A rather negative omen, the pitchfork indicates that trouble is on its way. Expect arguments, jealousies, anger and disputes.

♨ PLAITS

KEY MESSAGES: serendipity, intertwining, consequences

THE ORACLE SAYS: A plait is a reminder that we are never alone and that our lives intertwine with those of others. A coincidental meeting is not so full of serendipity…it is destiny at work.

♨ PLATYPUS

KEY MESSAGES: variety, a multi-talented person, skillful, secrecy

THE ORACLE SAYS: Success depends upon your ability to be adept at a variety of skills. Take the time to educate yourself and discover new ways of doing things. A person who is multi-talented may enter your work sphere.

ADDITIONAL INSIGHTS: A platypus on the bottom of the cup indicates a secret that is yet to be uncovered.

☕ POLICE

KEY MESSAGES: legal matters, justice

THE ORACLE SAYS: Justice will be done. Legal issues will be in your favour. If you have broken the law though, again expect justice to be done!

☕ PONY

KEY MESSAGES: ease, gentleness, an adventurous child

THE ORACLE SAYS: A pony in your cup shows you that things will now get easier for you. You will experience a quiet gentleness in your day-to-day life, which was not there previously.

☕ POMEGRANATE

KEY MESSAGES: death, winter, emotions, beliefs

THE ORACLE SAYS: When we decide we want a better life, often it is useful to examine our current belief systems and decide if there is any old thinking that is standing in our way. If so, this is the time to release our Selves from these old patterns and step up into what we now want.

ADDITIONAL INSIGHTS: A pomegranate on the bottom of your cup may signify a death, either literal or symbolic.

☕ POPPY

KEY MESSAGES: success, jealousy, dreams, reduction of pain

THE ORACLE SAYS: A poppy sprouting from your cup indicates a bright future, particularly career–wise. It may also coincide with the fulfillment of a long held wish.

ADDITIONAL INSIGHTS: If the poppy is on the bottom of the cup or has a broken stem, it indicates that others are jealous of your success. If the poppy shares the cup with symbols relating to health, it may indicate some health concerns.

☕ POSSUM

KEY MESSAGES: dexterity, curiosity, night

THE ORACLE SAYS: Curious possums can climb just about anything and some species can leap and glide from tree to tree. The same kind of faith and dexterity is being asked of you here. Keep your eyes open and your heart and mind flexible.

☕ POSTAGE STAMP

KEY MESSAGES: official communication, love letter

THE ORACLE SAYS: You will receive an official communication via mail, most probably of a legal nature. Alternatively, if the rest of the symbols in the cup lean towards relationship issues, you may well be on the receiving end of a love letter!

☕ POSTMAN

KEY MESSAGES: messages via mail

THE ORACLE SAYS: A postman situated close to the bottom of your cup means that the news that you await will be a long time coming. The closer your friendly postal worker is to the top of your cup, the faster your news will arrive.

☕ POWERLINES / CABLES

KEY MESSAGES: connectedness, support

THE ORACLE SAYS: Powerful people will be your allies in your current project. Monetary and psychological support will be available to you. Spiritually, you will feel more connected to the Universe and therefore more confident in your undertakings.

☕ PRAM

KEY MESSAGES: support, children

THE ORACLE SAYS: The ideas and dreams you have are in their infancy right now, but you will get the support that you need to grow them. Children may feature strongly in your life or unexpectedly during a trip.

☕ PREGNANCY

KEY MESSAGES: fertility, incubation of ideas, creativity

THE ORACLE SAYS: A pregnant figure can certainly suggest a conception for you or another person, but it's more likely to indicate that you are growing and incubating an idea or two. These ideas will generate much prosperity.

☕ PRETZEL

KEY MESSAGES: complexity, many obstacles

THE ORACLE SAYS: You have chosen the long way round haven't you? Stop, reassess and simplify. Things will run more smoothly if you do.

☕ PRIEST

KEY MESSAGES: formal religious ceremony, a blessing, forgiveness

THE ORACLE SAYS: You will shortly be invited to or attending a Christening, wedding, coming of age ceremony or funeral. Depending on the other symbols in the cup, this may be a reminder that it's time for forgiveness on your part towards someone else.

☕ PRIESTESS

KEY MESSAGES: intuition, magic, self-realisation, a journey off the beaten track

THE ORACLE SAYS: There is a deep and lasting wisdom in each of us and its manifestation is our intuition. Use this innate guide to make your decision.

☕ PUMPKIN

KEY MESSAGES: transformation, winter, Halloween

THE ORACLE SAYS: If a pumpkin appears in your cup it suggests the time is right to make that change that you have been intending. Change jobs, style, partners, hairdressers, homes...whatever you wish to transform, now is the time.

☕ PUPPET

KEY MESSAGES: manipulation, trickery

THE ORACLE SAYS: Seeing a puppet in your cup is an ill omen. It indicates that all is not what it seems. Someone is manipulating a situation behind the scenes.

☕ PUPPY

KEY MESSAGES: innocence, blind loyalty, trust

THE ORACLE SAYS: There will be someone entering your life who truly is an innocent. They may easily be taken advantage of if you do not intervene. Similarly, there may be a situation where loyalty or deep trust is involved. It is important to fully assess the situation in order to ensure you do not misguidedly offer these valuable gifts.

PURSE

KEY MESSAGES: money, debt/profit

THE ORACLE SAYS: A purse is an indicator of monetary worth and cash flow. A fat or full looking purse indicates that money will be plentiful. A small purse or one that looks open signifies that money or cash flow will be tighter.

ADDITIONAL INSIGHTS: A purse at the bottom of the cup indicates that money may be scarce.

PYRAMID

KEY MESSAGES: longevity, remembrance, ancient wisdom, Egypt

THE ORACLE SAYS: Rising out of the ancient sands of the desert, the pyramids still symbolise longevity and long life. Built to last forever, a pyramid also signifies a long memory or a great legacy.

♨ QUEEN

KEY MESSAGES: a powerful woman, a successful partnership, alliances

THE ORACLE SAYS: A well-connected female will enter your sphere of influence and will support you towards your desires. You may form a strong alliance which will ensure dynamic progress in business or career.

♨ QUESTION MARK

KEY MESSAGES: doubt, curiosity

THE ORACLE SAYS: If you have a nagging doubt about what is occurring, voice your concern. Look at a situation with curiosity and a sense of adventure. You never know what you will discover.

♨ QUILL

KEY MESSAGES: signing an important document, writing, an author or journalist

THE ORACLE SAYS: The writing arts are indicated here, with a focus on putting pen to paper. Always wanted to write that book? Now may well be a good time to start.

☕ RABBIT

KEY MESSAGES: fertility, sex, growth, renewal, Easter

THE ORACLE SAYS: The rabbit has been a symbol of fertility in many cultures and heralds a period of strong growth in your life. Whether it is more business ideas, more opportunities or even the conception of a child, you can expect rampant fertility. For those of you who are single, you will welcome a hot affair. For those who are partnered, a renewed interest in all things carnal will delight you. Enjoy!

☕ RAIL

KEY MESSAGES: steady, support, guidance

THE ORACLE SAYS: Steady she goes. Do not change your plans as they are the right strategy to begin with. Keep progressing. Know that you are being guided well.

☕ RAIN

KEY MESSAGES: cleansing, nourishing, new start, obstacles

THE ORACLE SAYS: You are being given the opportunity to start afresh. This new start allows you the benefit of hindsight. Examine carefully what went wrong last time and avoid the same mistakes.

ADDITIONAL INSIGHTS: If there is a rain pattern at the bottom of your cup, this may indicate a delay in the completion of a project or contract.

☕ RAINBOW

KEY MESSAGES: happiness, good fortune, money

THE ORACLE SAYS: Ah, a happy ending is in the cups for you! The question that you have asked of the Oracle, will be answered positively and things will work out better than you expected. If it is increased income flow that you require you will soon find a way to ensure this.

☕ RAT

KEY MESSAGES: strategic, suspicion, desertion

THE ORACLE SAYS: Just as a rat leaves a sinking ship, there is someone around you who is not in it for the long haul. They are simply biding their time for a better offer. This person is also highly strategic, so to get the better of them, you will need to out manoeuvre them. Think with your mind, not with your heart, to come out on top.

☕ RAVEN

KEY MESSAGES: spirituality, messages, news from afar

THE ORACLE SAYS: The big, black and beautiful raven has a misaligned reputation as a harbinger of ill news. Not so, unless the raven sits at the bottom of your cup. Should this powerful omen be placed elsewhere, it signals good news from afar or an invitation to look to the Spirit for advice or nourishment. This may be a good time to begin to meditate or deepen an existing spiritual practice.

☕ RECTANGLE

KEY MESSAGES: boxed in, funeral, mail

THE ORACLE SAYS: Discovering a rectangle that is solid indicates a feeling of restriction and prohibition. You are being advised to stretch out and change the cause of this feeling. If the rectangle is simply lines, this may indicate that you will be attending a funeral in the near future.

☕ REPTILE (also see Lizard, Snake)

KEY MESSAGES: distrust, disloyalty, cold-heartedness

THE ORACLE SAYS: Seeing a reptile in your cup normally indicates the presence of someone who cares little for the feelings of others and will act only for their own benefit. This person is not to be trusted and you must act accordingly.

☕ RHINOCEROS

KEY MESSAGES: shortsighted, male lover, sex

THE ORACLE SAYS: A man who is very sexual and potent will enter your life shortly. If men are not your preference, then a definite 'heating' of your sex life is certain.

ADDITIONAL INSIGHTS: If the rhino is on the bottom of your cup you are being warned not to be so shortsighted. Consider the long-term consequences of the situation.

☕ RICE

KEY MESSAGES: prosperity, purity, wedding

THE ORACLE SAYS: Rice in your cup is a wonderful omen indicating an increase in prosperity and happy times ahead. Rice is also a traditional omen for marriage, so expect an invitation to a wedding or even a marriage proposal for yourself!

☕ RING

KEY MESSAGES: commitment, wholeness, loyalty

THE ORACLE SAYS: If you are seeking a commitment in your relationship, possibly a marriage, a ring in your cup will predict this. You can be sure of loyalty and utmost trust in this relationship. If your question is more concerning a project or business, know that loyalty of the people around you or that of your customers is of paramount importance.

☕ RIPPLE

KEY MESSAGES: consequences, disturbance

THE ORACLE SAYS: A ripple in your cup indicates that there will be far-reaching consequences to an event or action that you are planning. Be very aware of each stakeholder's point of view before you act.

☕ RIVER

KEY MESSAGES: flow, surrender, spiritual assistance

THE ORACLE SAYS: To watch a river flow in your cup is to be asked to allow the same to happen in your life. Let go and let the Divine decide what will happen next. Surrender your fears, your worries and rest a while. You have done your very best to get yourself to this place. You will be taken care of.

☕ ROAD

KEY MESSAGES: long journey, change in direction, focus

THE ORACLE SAYS: There are many paths we can choose to travel and the one you are on now is soon to change. There will be a sudden change in direction, but fear not, this is not a negative journey. If you recall the times of greatest learning in your life, they most likely involved a major change of direction which resulted in a new focus. Get excited, as this brings new adventure, new people and new opportunities.

 ROOSTER

KEY MESSAGES: awareness, ignorance, pride

THE ORACLE SAYS: Wake up! You have been asleep for far too long. You have not been paying attention and your lack of vigilance could cost you dearly. For example, you might like to check the fine print on contracts, listen out for malicious gossip about you or take a long, hard look at your current behaviour.

ADDITIONAL INSIGHTS: If the rooster is at the bottom of your cup, it is a warning to not let pride get in the way of the right decision. Also, if the rooster is placed with other negative omens in the cup, it heralds a warning to avoid involvement with a business venture or high profile person.

ROPE

KEY MESSAGES: escape/entrapment, attraction, capture

THE ORACLE SAYS: A rope in your cup, particularly in the shape of a lasso, indicates that you are attempting to bring something towards you. You may or may not be aware of this magnetic attraction…which could be a good or bad thing. In this case you must be mindful of the other omens in your coffee cup. What is it that you are capturing? If it is something that you do not want to attract in your life, take sure action now to be rid of it.

ROSE

KEY MESSAGES: love, secret admirer, mothering, success

THE ORACLE SAYS: A rose blooming in your cup is an omen foretelling of a great love and success. If you are single, chances are you have a secret admirer who is far too shy to let their feelings be known. For those already lucky in love, expect your relationship to gather momentum and to celebrate a success in career or study.

ROWBOAT

KEY MESSAGES: effort, stamina, time, patience

THE ORACLE SAYS: A goal that you wish to accomplish may take more time and effort than first thought. Do not give up though, as things will move along slowly but surely. This is simply a patience issue.

☕ RUINS

KEY MESSAGES: dreams, efforts, foundations, ancient history

THE ORACLE SAYS: Seeing ruins in a cup heralds a great fall from grace. What dreams or projects were once alive are now broken and full of dust. However, all is not lost. From ruins great structures can be built. Work from solid foundations, exercise the wisdom that comes from hindsight and construct something new and different.

ADDITIONAL INSIGHTS: If ruins appear with symbols relating to love or relationships, it indicates that this marriage or affair is over. Start afresh, rather than try to revive something that is ancient history.

☕ SADDLE

KEY MESSAGES: stability, control, balance

THE ORACLE SAYS: There is an immediate need to take control of a situation in an assertive yet calm fashion. There is no need for aggression, just gentle, balanced and deliberate interaction which leads the situation where you want it to go.

ADDITIONAL INSIGHTS: If the image in the cup is a horse which has a clear saddle, this indicates that the freedom that you are enjoying has definite costs.

☕ SAFE

KEY MESSAGES: unsafe secrets, breach of confidentiality, secrecy

THE ORACLE SAYS: Sometimes it is prudent to keep quiet about a project or idea when it is in its infancy. Too often, our grandest plans are thwarted by others before they can mature and grow strong, so it is best to keep these heartfelt intentions in the 'safe' just for now. If you are involved in business, there is an indication that someone may be giving away information that you would prefer remain within the business.

☕ SAGE

KEY MESSAGES: wisdom, learning through past experiences, someone older who offers good advice.

THE ORACLE SAYS: You are being asked to recall your past experiences or consult someone with more experience than you to offer a solution. The sage leaf indicates that the answers lie in wisdom gained through age and self knowledge.

 SAIL

KEY MESSAGES: progress, new direction, new horizons

THE ORACLE SAYS: The winds of change are now blowing through your life, freeing you from that frustrating feeling of being stuck in stagnant waters. Things will now begin to move and flow.

SAND

KEY MESSAGES: time, being overwhelmed, slow progress

THE ORACLE SAYS: You may be feeling that time is either running too fast or too slow. Either way, this makes you feel overwhelmed and uneasy. It is important for your own peace of mind to rationally re-examine your workload and the way you balance work and family in particular.

 SAUSAGES

KEY MESSAGES: an impromptu party, a childlike person, simple pleasures

THE ORACLE SAYS: Remember how much fun you had at birthday parties when you were a kid? Or how much enjoyment a cheap and cheerful BBQ with friends can generate? Relax, open your mind and heart to your inner child and laugh a little by connecting with the simpler things in life.

 SAW

KEY MESSAGES: severing a powerful connection, harmful gossip

THE ORACLE SAYS: Be aware that a powerful connection, perhaps one that has been in existence for some time will be severed. This may or may not be a positive occurrence but being aware of its demise is important to you. Be careful not to engage in useless gossip about another as the consequences may come back to you threefold.

SAXOPHONE

KEY MESSAGES: a heady romantic relationship, a sexy encounter

THE ORACLE SAYS: Get ready to get knocked off your feet…you will soon experience a love affair that will be unusually sexually charged. If you already have a partner, you may be surprised by his or her lustful attitude. Or maybe you have been inspired to blow the cobwebs from your relationship and bring back the great sex!

☕ SCALES

KEY MESSAGES: justice, balance, fair exchange, person born under the sign of Libra (born between 24th September and 23rd October), legal matters

THE ORACLE SAYS: Natural justice rules all things, so be aware that justice will be done whether or not you see it. Be mindful of your actions and ensure that any legal involvement is engaged for the right reasons rather than out of revenge or spite. Balance and moderation in all aspects of life is being called for right now.

ADDITIONAL INSIGHTS: If the scales appear at the bottom of your cup, a protracted legal battle may occur.
For Fish Scales please see Fish.

☕ SCARECROW

KEY MESSAGES: Things are not what they seem, an empty threat

THE ORACLE SAYS: Your fear is unfounded. Release your fear and your over-developed defenses, as you are truly secure and protected.

☕ SCEPTRE

KEY MESSAGES: power, authority, recognition

THE ORACLE SAYS: You will be recognised for your achievements, and new responsibilities and power will be passed to you. You may soon become an authority in your place of work or take on a leadership role in your family or community.

SCISSORS

KEY MESSAGES: cutting of ties, a disagreement, endings

THE ORACLE SAYS: You may be the instigator of an argument or disagreement with a key figure in your life. This is a necessary debate and you should be careful to keep to the subject. A cutting of ties may be necessary for a time, to encourage personal wholeness.

SCOOTER

KEY MESSAGES: a quick decision, an independent view

THE ORACLE SAYS: Now is not the time for teamwork. The decision is yours and yours alone. Make your decision promptly and communicate it well.

SCORPIO

KEY MESSAGES: a person born under the sign of Scorpio (24th October and 22nd November), self-confidence, self-esteem, mystery, poison

THE ORACLE SAYS: The essence of Scorpio is one of power and confidence. The message here is to love who you are and know thyself. If you are wronged, protect your boundaries but be mindful not to delve into the realm of revenge.

☕ SCORPION

KEY MESSAGES: an unexpected betrayal, a person born under the sign of Scorpio (24th October and 22nd November) may become prominent in your life
KEY MESSAGES: You may experience a betrayal from someone you least expect. There may be a secret 'sting in the tail' of a contract…read all the fine print.

☕ SCUBA DIVER

KEY MESSAGES: depth, hidden emotions, surrender, scuba diving

THE ORACLE SAYS: You are being advised to take a deeper approach rather than just 'skim the surface'. Be sure to examine your real motives for doing something. Surrender your fears and go with the flow.

☕ SCYTHE

KEY MESSAGES: reap what you sow, the death of something, illness

THE ORACLE SAYS: The death of something is near. This is not necessarily a negative experience but can herald in a new beginning. You or someone you know may experience an illness particularly in the short term.

ADDITIONAL INSIGHTS: A scythe on the bottom of the cup means you may experience a grieving due to a forced separation.

☕ SEAGULL

KEY MESSAGES: freedom, a storm is coming

THE ORACLE SAYS: Seagulls are survivors of the storms that the great sea can generate. Similarly, you may soon experience a storm of your own, yet you will not only survive it, but flourish from it. This will give you a feeling of great expansion and freedom.

☕ SEESAW

KEY MESSAGES: decision-making, uneven fortunes

THE ORACLE SAYS: Stop changing your mind and decide what your position on a subject really is. There may be a period of unevenness, of 'ups and downs' in the near future. Keep your equilibrium!

☕ SEVEN

KEY MESSAGES: luck, income generation

THE ORACLE SAYS: Seven is a lucky number and you will be experiencing great luck particularly in matters of money and business.

☕ SEX

KEY MESSAGES: lust, connection, new experiences, trust/distrust

THE ORACLE SAYS: Seeing an image of a sexual nature in your cup carries no shame! This is a signal for you to examine your beliefs around trust or distrust of others and of your relationship with the world. Do you believe that you can passionately connect with the world safely? That you can trust others easily? That trying new things is an exciting prospect?

☕ SHAMROCK

KEY MESSAGES: luck, Ireland, happiness and good health

THE ORACLE SAYS: It's not just the leprechauns who believe that shamrocks bless the finder with lashings of good luck, happiness and good health…you'll soon believe it too!

SHELL

KEY MESSAGES: fertility, messages from the spirit world, shelter

THE ORACLE SAYS: Fertility of all kinds is being bestowed upon you. Expect greater creativity, better income or even a pregnancy.

SHARK

KEY MESSAGES: unknown dangers, dishonesty

THE ORACLE SAYS: This is a time to be wary of others' motives. You may not be seeing the real motive behind the need to do a deal or forge a relationship.

SHEEP

KEY MESSAGES: contentment, gullibility

THE ORACLE SAYS: There is great contentment waiting for you after a struggle. Perhaps you have forgotten how peaceful this feeling is and may not relax into your newfound contentment for some time. Look to your substantial reserves of natural wisdom and investigate the truth of a claim before making a decision.

SHEPHERD

KEY MESSAGES: a good leader, a mentor, a coach

THE ORACLE SAYS: You may be asked to step up and become a mentor for someone. Alternatively, someone who is a worthy leader will enter your life and be extremely motivating. Great care may be shown towards you.

SHIP

KEY MESSAGES: journey by sea, news from overseas, a journey of self-discovery

THE ORACLE SAYS: Set sail for the most important trip you will ever make...that towards your own self-knowledge. The time is ripe for an adventure into your inner Self.

ADDITIONAL INSIGHTS: If there are a number of ships or if the ship looks war–like, get ready for trouble.

SHOE

KEY MESSAGES: effort, physical labour, change

THE ORACLE SAYS: A project is going to take some dedicated effort to complete. Set yourself small, achievable deadlines to make the labour less strenuous.

SHOVEL/SPADE

KEY MESSAGES: recovery, taking responsibility

THE ORACLE: It is extremely healing to take responsibility for our part in a 'negative' situation and pave the way for recovery and wholeness.

☕ SIX

KEY MESSAGES: the number six will be significant in some way, home life, domestic matters

THE ORACLE SAYS: If there is a choice between home and elsewhere…choose home. All matters domestic and home related need your attention. It's a good time for a spring clean. The number six may be a 'lucky' number or play a significant role in a negotiation of some kind.

☕ SKELETON

KEY MESSAGES: age, death, the past, something hidden

THE ORACLE SAYS: A revelation from the past will be exposed. Death and age come forward as an issue. Are you concerned with aging or death? Do you feel that as you age you are somehow less in society? Is death really something you should be afraid of? The skeleton is here to remind you that death and aging are simply change and transformation.

☕ SKIS

KEY MESSAGES: speed, ease

THE ORACLE SAYS: The pace of your life will soon quicken. You will successfully traverse the mountains of responsibility that you are facing.

☕ SKULL

KEY MESSAGES: mortality, wisdom

THE ORACLE SAYS: Do not be afraid of physical death. Death is a natural part of life and is not the end but a transformation. Think about what your legacy may be after you eventually pass. What wisdom will you leave behind?

ADDITIONAL INSIGHTS: If you see a skull and crossbones (the pirate's symbol) take care that others do not steal your ideas or plunder your finances.

☕ SLED

KEY MESSAGES: smooth progress for a team, speedy resolution

THE ORACLE SAYS: If you are working in a team environment the sled signifies that quick and easy progress will be made towards your goal. This is not the time to go it alone.

☕ SMOKE

KEY MESSAGES: pay attention, camouflage

THE ORACLE SAYS: You are being asked to pay attention right now. There may be a cover up or a 'smokescreen' constructed, so that the truth remains hidden.

☕ SNAKE

KEY MESSAGES: intuition, malice/benevolence, the unification of male and female energies

THE ORACLE SAYS: A snake appearing, particularly in the mid-section of the cup, indicates a power male/female connection. This may not necessarily be a romantic connection (although it often is) but a meeting of great creative power. It can also signify a person entering your life who is either extremely beneficial or one filled with great spite. You will know them when you meet them!

☕ SNOW

KEY MESSAGES: blessings, soft landings

THE ORACLE SAYS: You have supporters from unknown quarters. You have presumed wrongly that the end of a relationship or association will be devastating to you. The landing will be softer than you thought.

☕ SPEAR

KEY MESSAGES: sorrow/achievement of goals, heartache

THE ORACLE SAYS: Relating to questions of love, a spear appearing without any other positive symbols indicates a breakup and much heartache. Appearing with positive symbols, the spear signifies that focus and realisation of a wish.

☕ SPADES (as in cards)

KEY MESSAGES: struggle, physical plane, groundedness

THE ORACLE SAYS: The solution to your issue is more physical than cerebral. You may encounter some resistance or even struggle towards a goal, but you will overcome this with dogged persistence.

☕ SPARROW

KEY MESSAGES: happiness, cheerfulness, positivity

THE ORACLE SAYS: Smile, the chirpy sparrow is here to reiterate that all is well. You will experience a period of great happiness with a flow of good luck.

ADDITIONAL INSIGHTS: If the sparrow is at the bottom of the cup, and in particular if it's surrounded by a cloud or a castle, this normally indicates that a person in high office or in authority will be undone by something quite simple that they did not forsee.

☕ SPIDER

KEY MESSAGES: connection, good fortune, environmentalism

THE ORACLE SAYS: Never fear a spider in your coffee cup! You will enjoy greater connection with all around you, particularly with your local community or with the Earth itself should you choose. There should be definite increases in your prosperity and fewer bills over the next few months.

☕ SPHINX

KEY MESSAGES: overcoming a challenge, discovery.

THE ORACLE SAYS: The legends of the sphinx often involved the setting and solving of puzzles. You are more than up to the challenge of solving the problems that present themselves. The answers are simpler than you think.

☕ SPIRIT

KEY MESSAGES: other-worldly assistance, fears from unknown sources

THE ORACLE SAYS: You are not alone. You are being supported and loved by those in Spirit. Do not fear things that may never happen. Continual worry is just bubblegum for the mind...it has no nourishment and gives you little satisfaction.

☕ SPOON

KEY MESSAGES: an offer of help, answers, a new baby

THE ORACLE SAYS: Thankfully, you will be given the help you need with little effort on your side. The answer to your query is on its way. Get ready for the arrival of a new baby and you may be asked to have some special responsibilities towards this child.

☕ SQUARE

KEY MESSAGES: lateral thinking, a new way, protection

THE ORACLE SAYS: Don't be boxed in! It is time to think and act creatively. If you have been feeling stuck and stagnant, now is the time to get moving! Act now!

☕ SQUIRREL

KEY MESSAGES: Forward planning, foresight, a playful individual

THE ORACLE SAYS: Whilst it's a fine thing to stay in the moment, it is also important to plan for the future or to have a contingency plan should things go astray. You are being reminded to think ahead and be prepared.

☕ STAG

KEY MESSAGES: power (particularly masculine), honour, an unattached male

THE ORACLE SAYS: You will be close to or will feel the massive strength and honour of male energy at its best. Security, protection, athleticism, wisdom... all through the gentle self assuredness of a positive male mentor, teacher or lover.

ADDITIONAL INSIGHTS: If the stag is at the bottom of the cup, you may encounter a male who is merely out for some sexual fun, nothing more. How you deal with this is up to you!

STAR

KEY MESSAGES: good health, recognition, reward, love

THE ORACLE SAYS: A twinkling star shining brightly from your cup is a wonderful omen of good health, good fortune and love increasing from all directions. You are being rewarded for a job well done.

ADDITIONAL INSIGHTS: A star on the bottom of the cup may signify that recognition at work will not be forthcoming and that your luck may be running out in a particular situation.

STEPS

KEY MESSAGES: progression, advancement.

THE ORACLE SAYS: You are closer to your wish than you have ever been and you are continually advancing towards what you desire. Do not be concerned about timeframe, you are making steady progress.

 STICKS

KEY MESSAGES: negativity, disagreement, bad news

THE ORACLE SAYS: Sticks that are crossed over each other signify that a series of arguments and disagreements with serious consequences. If the sticks are made into any recognisable 'stick figure' this indicates bad news.

STRAWBERRY

KEY MESSAGES: the time is right, a favourable offer, lust

THE ORACLE SAYS: If the luscious strawberry appears in your cup get ready for a juicy proposal, offer or a lusty new relationship. The time is ripe to say 'yes' to an offer that seems dreamlike in its perfection.

SUITCASE

KEY MESSAGES: travel, escape, moving house, a visitor

THE ORACLE SAYS: Whether you travel, change your address or accept a visitor into your home, a change is on the horizon! Refresh your mind, body and spirit by looking closely at things that are new or seeing a situation through the eyes of someone else.

 **SUN**

KEY MESSAGES: good health, positive outlook, improved outlook

THE ORACLE SAYS: Expect radiant health and a sunny outlook on life. You are positioned well for growth and future happiness.

ADDITIONAL INSIGHTS: A sun on the bottom of the cup indicates less than perfect health or an event that has occurred in the past which has caused negative consequences.

 **SWALLOW**

KEY MESSAGES: freedom, happiness, increased fortune, lifting of a burden

THE ORACLE SAYS: A bluebird of happiness is sweeping down over your cup, indicating much lighter and brighter circumstances. A burden lifts and it is time to enjoy life again.

 **SWAN**

KEY MESSAGES: royalty, transformation, disguise, grace

THE ORACLE SAYS: Like the ugly duckling who turned in to a swan, there is a metamorphosis taking place. You may not see this transformation at first but know that the change is a positive and graceful one.

ADDITIONAL INSIGHTS: A swan at the bottom of the cup indicates a romantic separation.

☕ SWORD

KEY MESSAGES: action, urgency, warrior-energy, defense

THE ORACLE SAYS: Stop your procrastination and act now. There may be a need to defend yourself, a member of your family, or a friend over an issue that seemingly had insignificant beginnings. Should you do need to use your power for protection, ensure this is done with honour and with cleverness, avoiding aggression.

ADDITIONAL INSIGHTS: A sword that looks broken indicates a bitter argument or a defeat.

☕ TABLE

KEY MESSAGES: honesty, openness

THE ORACLE SAYS: It is time to put all your cards on the table and be honest with someone or with yourself. This is not the time for reservations. Clarity and honesty are called for to resolve a potentially explosive situation. Be mindful of other symbols in the cup. For example, other symbols relating to a particular person may indicate the need to discuss things clearly with them.

☕ TACK

KEY MESSAGES: painful, sharp, smartness

THE ORACLE SAYS: You need all your wits about you as it's intelligence and sharp thinking that will bring you the greatest success.

ADDITIONAL INSIGHTS: If the tack is on the bottom of your cup, take care! An accident that is not serious – but painful – may slow you down somewhat.

☕ TALON

KEY MESSAGES: capture, unexpected control

THE ORACLE SAYS: A bird of prey swoops down and captures its prey with the deathly grip of its mighty talons. Its greatest weapon is surprise. Ensure that you are not caught out unexpectedly, in particular by someone with more authority than you. An example of this kind of person may be a teacher or a boss.

 TANK

KEY MESSAGES: solidarity, preparation

THE ORACLE SAYS: There may be wars ahead. The best strategy is to be super prepared and to have your team close.

 TAP

KEY MESSAGES: focus/diluted, creativity, money

THE ORACLE SAYS: Is the tap you see dripping? If so you are wasting your talents, your money or your effort. If the tap is drip-free, expect a flow of money, ideas and connections on tap.

TAURUS (astrological symbol is a bull)

KEY MESSAGES: Someone born between 21st April and 21st May.

THE ORACLE SAYS: Earth-loving and grounded, Taurean energy is warm and family-orientated. Sometimes stubborn, sometimes inflexible, the bull's horns often lock on money issues.

TAXI

KEY MESSAGES: out of control, concealed

THE ORACLE SAYS: When you take a taxi, some one else drives you to your destination. Right now, in life, you may be feeling uncomfortable that others seem to have taken control of your destiny under the guise of assisting you. Remember the fact that when you take a taxi, someone else may be steering, but you are telling them where to go.

TEACUP/COFFEE CUP

KEY MESSAGES: attention, importance

THE ORACLE SAYS: If you are reading a coffee cup and a similar cup pops up as an omen, it is to further validate the importance of that particular reading.

TEAPOT

KEY MESSAGES: thoughtfulness, conversation, communication

THE ORACLE SAYS: Hungry for some stimulating conversation? Seeing a teapot in your cup indicates the need for greater socialising and the importance of getting together with like minds.

☕ TEAR

KEY MESSAGES: sadness, grief

THE ORACLE SAYS: There is great power in grief and in tears. Wash away your regrets and your old patterns. This can be a time of great spiritual progression.

☕ TELEPHONE (includes mobile phone)

KEY MESSAGES: communication, distance, wooing

THE ORACLE SAYS: Expect an important phone call. If this telephone has other omens relating to love near it, you may be wooed by telephone or take part in a passionate long distance relationship.

☕ TELEVISION

KEY MESSAGES: watching, objectivity, involvement

THE ORACLE SAYS: Objectivity is the issue here. You may be involved in mediating a dispute between parties. Perhaps you have been watching a situation to see how it turns out. Either way, there needs to be a balance between taking action and staying divorced completely from the situation. Look closely at your motives.

☕ TEMPLE

KEY MESSAGES: sacredness, sanctuary, honour

THE ORACLE SAYS: You are being summoned spiritually to treat your Self with more honour. A certain sacredness of your own purpose and intentions needs to be acknowledged and kept in sanctuary. You are a spiritual being enclosed in a beautiful functional body. If you have been treating our body with little respect by partying too hard or working hours that are far too long it is important now to make the healing of your body a priority.

☕ TENT

KEY MESSAGES: protection, short-term, back to nature, simplicity

THE ORACLE SAYS: Simplicity is the best course of action right now. Strip back any superfluous administration, decoration or planning. Time–wise, the issue you are consulting the Oracle about will be one that exists short term.

☕ THORN

KEY MESSAGES: problem person, persistence

THE ORACLE SAYS: There is a single person or issue which keeps reappearing to hamper your progress. If it is a person, their persistence is admirable. How do we remove this 'thorn in your side'? Find out this person's motives by acting directly. You may be surprised and a resolution may be swift.

 THREE

KEY MESSAGES: magic, wisdom, trinity, maiden/mother/crone, cycles

THE ORACLE SAYS: The number three is perhaps the most consistently magical number across many cultures. It signifies a gaining of wisdom, maturity and greater skill. You are being reminded that there is a natural cycle to all things, so do not be distressed if things seem a little chaotic at present.

THRONE

KEY MESSAGES: royalty, power, increased responsibility

THE ORACLE SAYS: You will be offered a position of greater power, but what it comes with is much greater responsibility and expectation. Be certain that you understand what this offer really means for you. At first examination it may seem exactly what you have been working so diligently toward, but are you fully prepared to give up aspects of your life that nourish you in a different way? Do not be afraid to negotiate.

THUMB

KEY MESSAGES: yes/no, positive/negative

THE ORACLE SAYS: If the thumb is facing upwards; the 'thumbs up,' this is a positive omen meaning 'yes'. If the thumb is facing downwards; the 'thumbs down', this indicates a negative response or a 'no' to your question.

 TIGER

KEY MESSAGES: energy, passion, surprises, money.

THE ORACLE SAYS: Seeing a magnificent tiger in your cup indicates a future filled with high energy, passion and prosperity. Feel confident to take a few business risks…you will come out on top.

ADDITIONAL INSIGHTS: If the tiger is crouching in the bottom of your cup, do take care that you don't pressure someone unnecessarily. They may decide to turn around and bite you and you will certainly not obtain the outcome that you seek.

TOAD

KEY MESSAGES: hidden motives, authenticity, story telling

THE ORACLE SAYS: Someone is not what they seem. In fact, there is a big gap between what they tell you and what they mean. Ensure you look for the true story.

☕ TOOTH

KEY MESSAGES: wisdom, challenge, dedication, longevity

THE ORACLE SAYS: Craving a challenge? Feeling restless? This tooth that has appeared in your coffee cup signifies a period of movement, learning and growth. Do not be afraid of the changes that will soon be upon you. After all, you have asked for them.

ADDITIONAL INSIGHTS: If the tooth is very high up in your cup or appears very large, this signals longevity.

☕ TORCH

KEY MESSAGES: clarity, illumination, inspiration

THE ORACLE SAYS: You are being invited to lead by example and you will not only succeed in your intention, but inspire others. You have an opportunity to show others the way things can be done with integrity and ease. There is a need for clarification in your business dealings.

☕ TOWER

KEY MESSAGES: example, display, isolation

THE ORACLE SAYS: Whether you realise it or not, you are being made an example of by someone that is in a more powerful position than you. There is a certain amount of manipulation present that you may not be conscious of, so if you are feeling a sense of isolation or injustice, speak out.

ADDITIONAL INSIGHTS: If the tower you view is crumbling or turning into ruins (also see Ruins), you may have unintentionally made an enemy though what you believed was a light throwaway comment. They did not see it that way.

 **TOY**

KEY MESSAGES: playful, children, youth

THE ORACLE SAYS: Too much work and not enough play makes one very dull indeed. It is playtime! Think about what you used to love to do as a child and consider doing it now. Was it drawing, running madly, dancing, petting your dog or building something? Just do it! A more youthful approach is needed to create something new and fresh.

ADDITIONAL INSIGHTS: If a toy sits on the bottom of your cup, it indicates that a more mature approach is needed. It might also indicate that someone is about to throw a tantrum more befitting a three-year-old!

TRAFFIC LIGHTS

KEY MESSAGES: preparation, stop/go

THE ORACLE SAYS: Be totally mindful that the project that you are working on may have a number of stops and starts. Take heart though, these pauses are for your own safety.

☕ TRAIN

KEY MESSAGES: journey, progression, goals

THE ORACLE SAYS: You have a clear goal in sight and although the journey will be over in quite some time, you will get there and be successful. You are on the right track.

☕ TRAY

KEY MESSAGES: rest, sickness

THE ORACLE SAYS: You may find yourself in bed either for a well-earned rest or, unfortunately, as a result of sickness.

☕ TREASURE CHEST

KEY MESSAGES: unexpected fortune, money, success

THE ORACLE SAYS: Pirates aren't the only ones to discover a treasure chest are they? Whatever it is that is your heart's desire, it will be coming to you faster than you thought. Material riches in particular are indicated by this omen.

TREE

KEY MESSAGES: healing, spirituality, strength, goals

THE ORACLE SAYS: Discovering a tree in your cup is a fine omen. It indicates strength of purpose and an attainment of goals. Spiritually, it indicates a seeking nature and someone who is flexible yet strong in their dealings with others. If you have been though an unpleasant or damaging situation recently, you are already beginning to heal. Spend more time in nature.

TRIANGLE

KEY MESSAGES: good/bad luck, achievement/failure, inclusion/exclusion

THE ORACLE SAYS: The shape of the triangle is an ancient omen which, dependant upon its direction, may indicate great or terrible things. If the triangles point is upwards, expect good fortune, the achievement of your set goals and social inclusion. If the point is facing downwards there may be a problem with money, bad luck, obstacles placed in the path of your dreams or your exclusion from a circle of friends or associates. If the triangle's point is to either side, look to the past (pointing left) or to the future (pointing right) for the answer to your query.

TRIDENT

KEY MESSAGES: sea, crossroads, decisions, options

THE ORACLE SAYS: You have come to a crossroads where there will be a number of options to choose from. All options should be considered carefully and weighed according to your future intentions. If the trident is pointing towards the rim, move forward with the most inventive, futuristic or creative solution. If the trident points downwards, the conservative option is the most prudent.

You may also be travelling over the sea or meeting someone whose job is working with the ocean.

☕ TROPHY

KEY MESSAGES: awards, recognition, rewards

THE ORACLE SAYS: You have been seen. You have done well. You will be rewarded for your effort and your personal power will increase.

☕ TRUCK

KEY MESSAGES: big, hard, tough, weighty

THE ORACLE SAYS: What ever it is that you are wishing to attempt, know that it will not be a light and easy task. Lots of hard work, big decisions and tough calls will be the way forward. However, you will get there!

☕ TRUMPET

KEY MESSAGES: an announcement, recognition, power

THE ORACLE SAYS: Prepare yourself for an announcement of great consequence to you or your family. This may well be a promotion, a birth, marriage announcement, or some high profile recognition for an accomplishment. This announcement will have far reaching consequences.

☕ TUNNEL

KEY MESSAGES: doubt, fear, hope, light

THE ORACLE SAYS: Yes, there is light at the end of your tunnel! Where you have felt lost and alone, the cups are here to advise that there is no need to question how things will turn out. You will feel lighter and happier as you move forward. Just keep going.

☕ TURKEY (also see Bird)

KEY MESSAGES: celebration, happiness, joy, Christmas/Thanksgiving, plentitude

THE ORACLE SAYS: You can look forward to a time when many of your family or friends are together for a celebration. This will be a very joyous time for all and there will none of the usual family tensions.

ADDITIONAL INSIGHTS: If the turkey dances at the bottom of your cup or is present with other negative omens, be prepared for a failure... something will 'be a turkey'.

☕ TURTLE

KEY MESSAGES: feminine energy, love, harmony, spiritual bliss

THE ORACLE SAYS: The gentle turtle, in particular the sea turtle, is a spiritual omen of great force. It indicates a return to love and harmonious conditions, and invites you to fully express your feminine power. If you are male, there is no shame in consciously choosing some of the feminine aspects such as attraction, creativity and compassion rather than the masculine equivalents of pushing, rationality and self-judgment.

☕ TUSK

KEY MESSAGES: great size, happiness, good luck, potent male

THE ORACLE SAYS: Feel your confidence swell! Expect good luck and happiness to rain upon you! If you are a single woman, you may well be surprised by the entry of a very keen suitor into your life. You will not miss this man…he will be passionate, potent and very enthusiastic.

☕ TWINS

KEY MESSAGES: A Gemini – someone who is born between 22nd May and 21st, mirror image, repetition

THE ORACLE SAYS: You may be repeating an old pattern yet again. Ensure that you have definitely learned your lesson from last time and you don't make the same mistake again.

ADDITIONAL INFORMATION: Should you see twins near the handle or at the three o'clock position, this may indicate the arrival of twins. This may be in the form of newborn babies or as grown twins.

☕ TWO

KEY MESSAGES: change, home, partnership

THE ORACLE SAYS: The number two in your cup normally precedes a major life change. This manifests most commonly as a change in the home such as moving house or the creation or dissolution of a partnership. Check the other omens in your cup for more clues.

UFO

KEY MESSAGES: curiosity, surprises, technological breakthrough

THE ORACLE SAYS: A flying saucer in your coffee cup is pointing you towards developing a great sense of discovery and curiosity. For those of you who are involved in technical or scientific projects here is a good chance that you will make a major and quite unexpected breakthrough.

UMBRELLA

KEY MESSAGES: protection, support, health

THE ORACLE SAYS: You can trust that you will be protected and supported through out a difficult time. The offer of support is a genuine one.

ADDITIONAL INSIGHTS: If the umbrella is slightly closed or at the bottom of your cup, watch your health. A check-up is advised.

UNICORN

KEY MESSAGES: intuition, creative freedom, love, magic

THE ORACLE SAYS: Relax your conscious rational mind and allow your intuition to blossom. Your decision-making will be far superior if you listen to your inner wisdom than if you just use your logic alone. For those in creative jobs, you will be allowed much more creative freedom than ever before which should enable outstanding results. For those who are single, you will receive a romantic approach by someone who seems quite dreamy, but is very clear in their erotic intent.

VALLEY

KEY MESSAGES: setback, obstacles

THE ORACLE SAYS: You will face a setback whilst reaching for your goal. Don't despair though, you will pass through this valley soon enough and make your way back to higher ground.

VAMPIRE

KEY MESSAGES: draining, boundaries, energy zapping, manipulation

THE ORACLE SAYS: Who is it that is sucking you dry? What part of your life no longer serves you, yet you do it and it drains you of life and enthusiasm? Are your personal boundaries solid enough that you can say 'no' without guilt or regret? Take a deep look at these questions and answer honestly. You are being challenged to rid yourself of activities and people who drain your energy for their own purposes. Stop being a doormat and focus on what you want and need to be happy and healthy.

ADDITIONAL INSIGHTS: If the vampire is hovering at the bottom of your cup it also may indicate someone who wishes to sexually dominate you or is highly possessive.

VEGETABLES

KEY MESSAGES: plenty, good health, money

THE ORACLE SAYS: If you see vegetables in your cup expect a time of material prosperity. Money will be flowing towards you as will the gifts it can buy. Robust good health is also indicated.

☕ VINE

KEY MESSAGES: complexity, plenty, indulgence, entanglements in love

THE ORACLE SAYS: If the vine should appear on its own in your cup, it heralds prosperity and feasting. In fact, it may even signal overindulgence if you aren't careful! If the vine winds its way along with other symbols alluding to love or relationships, it indicates that you will be highly attracted to more than one person which may cause some unnecessary entanglement.

☕ VIOLIN

KEY MESSAGES: outstanding success, excellence, fame, a musician

THE ORACLE SAYS: Even if you are not musical, seeing a violin in your cup is usually a wonderful omen indicating success and recognition. This recognition may even extend to fame. For those that are musical or earn their living musically, you will receive greater positive notoriety from your performances.

ADDITIONAL INSIGHTS: If the violin is at the base of the cup, you may fall victim to someone who is telling you a sob story that is not true. Do not misplace your compassion.

VIRGO (astrological symbol is the virgin)

KEY MESSAGES: a person born between 24th August and 23rd September may become important to you, perfectionism, excellence, precision

THE ORACLE SAYS: Now is the time to pay attention to detail and strive for the best you can do or afford. It is not a time to cut corners. Any extra time or money that is spent will not be wasted.

VICE

KEY MESSAGES: pressure, negotiation

THE ORACLE SAYS: You may feel like you are being squeezed and pressured into something at present, and the vice in your cup validates this. Try to negotiate your way out of the situation or just don't play at all

VOLCANO

KEY MESSAGES: anger, fire, resolution, relief

THE ORACLE SAYS: How long will it take before you can express how you feel? Do you believe that expressing anger is a negative thing and best held inside? Perhaps you feel the opposite; that it is okay to rage at someone whenever you feel like it? A volcano in your cup is inviting you to look at the way anger plays out in your life. Healthy anger expressed with balance, with thought and with justice in mind. It is just as valid an emotion as happiness or love. Gain resolution and relief by confronting your misshapen ideas about anger.

☕ VULTURE

KEY MESSAGES: opportunist, death, grief, clearing

THE ORACLE SAYS: It is easy to dislike the vulture isn't it? They are not very pretty, they stalk the dying and they eat stinking carrion. But what of a world where things are not cleared and cleaned? Where death is not recognised as a part of life and grief is not expressed? A vulture in your cup signifies that there is still some grief to work through which will reduce your burden. Pick these bones clean and allow this clearing to occur and you will move forward towards your ideal life far quicker.

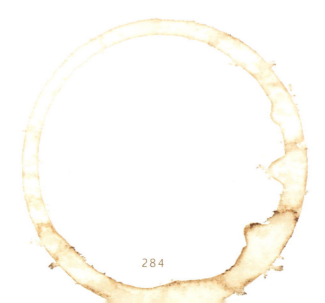

284

☕ WALKING STICK

KEY MESSAGES: an older person, support

THE ORACLE SAYS: You may be seeking physical, mental or financial support and this may be a source of great anxiety for you or someone in your family. A walking stick indicates that this help will be forthcoming and there will be someone to lean on.

☕ WALLET

KEY MESSAGES: money, finances

THE ORACLE SAYS: Seeing a wallet or purse in your cup always indicates an increase in the finance department. Should the wallet be open though, this shows that you will be paying out more than you are earning!

☕ WAND

KEY MESSAGES: magic, wishes granted, promises

THE ORACLE SAYS: Allow the Universe to wave its magic wand and grant you your wishes! If you haven't thought of something you want, now is the time to focus and ask. Also, if you make a promise to someone, this promise will be kept, even if you are ambivalent around it later.

☕ WARRIOR

KEY MESSAGES: fight, strategy, resilience, strength

THE ORACLE SAYS: You may have a fight on your hands or you may need to protect your interests. The honourable warrior is strategic and compassionate, shunning unnecessary aggression. You can be strong and resilient without causing unnecessary harm.

☕ WASP

KEY MESSAGES: minor insults, small obstacles

THE ORACLE SAYS: Although someone may sting you with their insults or loose tongue, really, they are of no consequence in the larger picture. Brush them off and get on with things.

☕ WATCH

KEY MESSAGES: timeliness, clock–watcher

THE ORACLE SAYS: The issue that you are enquiring about requires you to be very aware of the timeframe in which it exists. Time is important to the outcome.

☕ WATER

KEY MESSAGES: fluidity, freedom, emotions, journey over water

THE ORACLE SAYS: Traditionally, water signifies the emotional life. The kind of water that washes around our cup indicates the emotions you may be experiencing right now or in the future. Remember, ultimately, you are in control of how you feel and there is nothing that appears in a cup that cannot be changed or influenced.

ADDITIONAL INSIGHTS:

The ocean with large surf signifies some turbulent emotions, with some difficulties in keeping life balanced.

The ocean with small surf heralds less significant highs and lows and some very positive indications such as anticipation, joy and excitement.

A lake or still pond reflects more introverted and quiet emotions.

A river indicates a healthy flow or life, ideas, health and a continual source of spiritual sustenance.

☕ WATERFALL

KEY MESSAGES: risk, momentum, plenty

THE ORACLE SAYS: Whilst a waterfall signifies a period of plenty, it is earned through taking risks. A waterfall is also a sign of momentum, so things will certainly begin moving if you have felt any stagnancy in your life.

☕ WATERING CAN

KEY MESSAGES: creativity, nurturing

The Oracle Says: Care and nurturing is what your creative Self requires. It is often easy to criticise ourselves and think that we are not good enough. These negative thought patterns only serve to close up our creative source further. You are invited to allow your magnificence to flow.

☕ WEB (also see Spider)

Key Messages: connection, a trap, weaving

The Oracle Says: Fine threads of energy connect us all. You are being invited to examine the kinds of connective threads that you have woven. Are there some connections that are broken and threadbare? Are there some that are so thin they barely exist? Or some that are too thick and gnarled and therefore repressive? All of these need healing and reweaving.

Additional Insights: A web on the bottom of the cup can indicate a trap. Look carefully and do your research before an undertaking a major purchase or making an important decision.

☕ WEDDING CAKE

Key Messages: wedding, partnership

THE ORACLE SAYS: A wedding cake most often signifies the initiation of a marriage or a partnership. If the cake is surrounded by other positive omens that relate to finances, the partnership will be a profitable one.

☕ WELL

KEY MESSAGES: depth, creativity, wishes

THE ORACLE SAYS: Your deepest, most secret wish will be granted. The creative source is often represented by a well, so creative types in particular, need to be mindful not to not to empty the well too much. Creative energy needs to be replaced once drawn upon. This is the natural cycle of things.

☕ WHALE

KEY MESSAGES: greatness, unassuming strength, joy, large size

THE ORACLE SAYS: Mighty but supremely gentle, a whale in your cup is a powerful omen of impending greatness and joy. No matter how big the project is that you are attempting to tackle, you will be successful with a strategy of a quiet strength.

☕ WHEAT

KEY MESSAGES: happiness, fulfillment, prosperity

THE ORACLE SAYS: Wheat appearing in your coffee is a happy omen. Whether it be a single stalk or a bunch indicates strong prosperity. You will always have enough bread on your table.

 WHEEL

KEY MESSAGES: cycles, transport, progress

THE ORACLE SAYS: There are natural cycles to everything. The wheel of life continues moving through life, growth, death and transformation. A wheel also indicates travel in the short term. Pack your bags, you are headed out for a trip!

WHIP

KEY MESSAGES: subjugation, force, timeliness

THE ORACLE SAYS: In today's fast paced environment, it is tempting to drive yourself or others too hard. It is important that individual liberties and freedoms are respected particularly in the workplace. There should be no master/slave relationship at work with employers and employees.

 WINDMILL

KEY MESSAGES: preparation, natural energy, Dutch

THE ORACLE SAYS: Once built, a windmill harnesses large amounts of natural energy simply by going with the flow. You are being advised that the best way forward is to prepare and then allow. Do not push against the wind. You do not need to struggle.

☕ WINDOW

KEY MESSAGES: view, open, discovery, spiritual awakening

THE ORACLE SAYS: A new spirit of openness and clarity will breeze through your life. A point of view or an outlook that is new for you will be sunshine for your mind and heart.

☕ WINE GLASS

KEY MESSAGES: socialising, a party, a toast, a winemaker or sommelier

THE ORACLE SAYS: There are a number of parties on your social horizon so you may want to think about what you will be wearing! There may also be a getting together of people that you have not seen in some time. This will be a memorable occasion and it could celebrate a landmark such as a significant birthday or anniversary.

☕ WINGS

KEY MESSAGES: freedom, escape, messages, airforce

THE ORACLE SAYS: Like the god Hermes with his winged feet, a message of some importance is flying speedily to you.

☕ WISHBONE

KEY MESSAGES: wishes

THE ORACLE SAYS: A wishbone is a happy omen, letting you know that the wish that is top of mind will be granted.

☕ WITCH

KEY MESSAGES: wise, ancient spiritual practice, secrecy, weaving

THE ORACLE SAYS: Witches were the original wise women of the village and even the word witch comes from the same Old English word as weaver. A Witch in your cup signals a heightening in your wisdom and psychic development. Your abilities to weave the worlds together will improve over time if this is a path your wish to follow. A Witch can also signify the necessity to keep a matter quiet or secret.

☕ WIZARD

KEY MESSAGES: wisdom, ancient spiritual practice, masculine power

THE ORACLE SAYS: If a wizard casts a spell in your cup it is one to entice you to exercise your own considerable inner wisdom. Like finding a Witch in your cup, a wizard as an omen also encourages a greater spiritual connection with nature and the elements.

☕ WOLF

KEY MESSAGES: wisdom, protection, justified force, strategy

THE ORACLE SAYS: The much-maligned wolf is certainly not a bad omen if he walks around your cup. In many native cultures, the wolf is a symbol of just protection and force. The wolf is also an animal that invites you to use your strength and power wisely, with great regard for others.

ADDITIONAL INSIGHTS: A wolf on the base of your cup may indicate a cunning adversary.

☕ WOMAN

KEY MESSAGES: someone you recognise, feminine point of view

THE ORACLE SAYS: When you spot a woman in your cup look carefully to see whether you recognise her. If you do, or intuitively feel that it is someone you know this person will shortly play a greater role in your life. A figure of a woman also shows that a feminine perspective may be the most advantageous attitude to take.

ADDITIONAL INSIGHTS: If a woman appears on the bottom of the cup, this woman may not be a positive influence or she may be the bringer of bad news. Check carefully to see if you recognise any woman you know.

☕ WORM

KEY MESSAGES: earth, transformation, regeneration

THE ORACLE SAYS: The humble worm does all manner of great deeds in the garden. They enrich the soil. They aerate it and assist with regeneration. So if you are lucky enough to have a worm or two in your coffee, don't squirm, be excited. A period of growth, renewal and transformation will be occurring.

☕ WREATH

KEY MESSAGES: remembrance, recognition, Christmas

THE ORACLE SAYS: You will be lauded for a good deed or for a talent that you felt destined to hide. You may also be remembered fondly by someone that you haven't encountered for years. They may pave the way for you in a business situation or provide a reference or recommendation.

X

KEY MESSAGES: finding your destination, marking an event, an unknown person

THE ORACLE SAYS: Almost all cultures conduct rites of passage such as certain birthdays, marriages and deaths and they are marked by ritual or celebration. You are being reminded that it is important to mark an achievement or a particular point in your life so that you can better see how far you have progressed.

ADDITIONAL INSIGHTS: An X at the bottom of the cup indicates an unknown person or a person whose identity will remain a secret.

X–RAY

KEY MESSAGES: a need for transparency, honesty

THE ORACLE SAYS: You are being asked to exercise your ability to see through the surface motives of a newcomer. Honesty and knowledge is important at this time.

XYLOPHONE

KEY MESSAGES: a childlike personality, simplicity

THE ORACLE SAYS: We live in complex times and you are being reminded that often the simplest solution is the best. You may encounter a person who has a playful and childlike attitude. This person may bring the innocent joy of the young or the ignorance and stubbornness.

☕ YACHT

KEY MESSAGES: natural ability, financial success

THE ORACLE SAYS: Concentrate on what you are naturally talented at and develop this further. Financial success is highly likely.

☕ YARN

KEY MESSAGES: confusion, over complication

THE ORACLE SAYS: The appearance of a ball of yarn, wool or string indicates a tendency for confusion or unnecessary entanglements. Keep things simple and focused for best results.

☕ YOKE

KEY MESSAGES: subservience, duty, dominance

THE ORACLE SAYS: To be of service does not have to mean you are dominated. Consider the reasons you are tied to someone or something.

☕ YETI

KEY MESSAGES: wildness, a mystery, the Himalayas

THE ORACLE SAYS: Why do you fear your inherent wildness? An integral part of each of us is our natural, wild Self. You are called to remember that repressing this part of your true Self is an unhealthy path to tread.

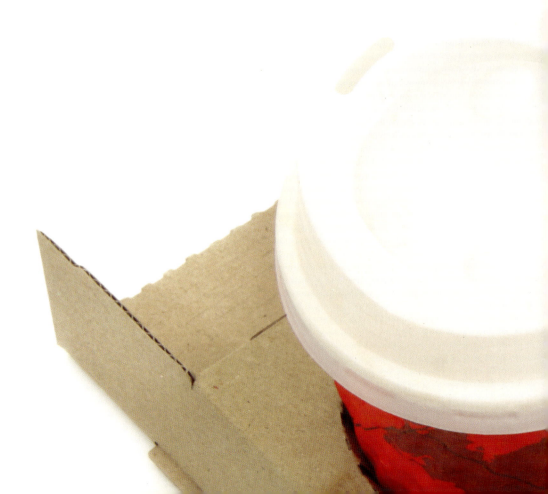

Z

KEY MESSAGES: rebellion, conquest

THE ORACLE SAYS: Like the dashing Zorro, you too can be a revolutionary – and a Z slashed across your cup calls you to action! This is not the time to play it safe! Be adventurous!

ZEBRA

KEY MESSAGES: uniqueness, Africa

THE ORACLE SAYS: Do you know that each and every zebra are marked differently. There are no two alike. The message for you here is one of individuality and uniqueness. There is great value in being different.

ZEPPELIN

KEY MESSAGES: difficulty in getting off the ground, delay, failure

THE ORACLE SAYS: A project you have set your sights on will not be easy to get off the ground and delays and general slowness will be the norm.

ADDITIONAL INSIGHTS: If the zeppelin is at the bottom of the cup, the project may fail entirely.

 ZIGGURAT

KEY MESSAGES: raising consciousness, path to wisdom

THE ORACLE SAYS: You desire a more satisfying spiritual experience and it is time to make this your priority. Put material things and administration aside for now and call upon the wisdom of your ancestors.

ZIPPER

KEY MESSAGES: discretion, silence, communicate less

THE ORACLE SAYS: Zipper up that mouth! Discretion or even total silence is what is being called for right now. This is also a reminder that gossip is not an ethical pastime.

Z

KEY MESSAGES: rebellion, conquest

THE ORACLE SAYS: Like the dashing Zorro, you too can be a revolutionary – and a Z slashed across your cup calls you to action! This is not the time to play it safe! Be adventurous!

ZEBRA

KEY MESSAGES: uniqueness, Africa

THE ORACLE SAYS: Do you know that each and every zebra are marked differently. There are no two alike. The message for you here is one of individuality and uniqueness. There is great value in being different.

ZEPPELIN

KEY MESSAGES: difficulty in getting off the ground, delay, failure

THE ORACLE SAYS: A project you have set your sights on will not be easy to get off the ground and delays and general slowness will be the norm.

ADDITIONAL INSIGHTS: If the zeppelin is at the bottom of the cup, the project may fail entirely.

☕ ZIGGURAT

KEY MESSAGES: raising consciousness, path to wisdom

THE ORACLE SAYS: You desire a more satisfying spiritual experience and it is time to make this your priority. Put material things and administration aside for now and call upon the wisdom of your ancestors.

☕ ZIPPER

KEY MESSAGES: discretion, silence, communicate less

THE ORACLE SAYS: Zipper up that mouth! Discretion or even total silence is what is being called for right now. This is also a reminder that gossip is not an ethical pastime.

Q AND A

ESPRESSO!

Here are some commonly asked questions about The Coffee Oracle and some concise replies that you may find useful.

Q: What if I don't see anything in my cup?
A: If you have really looked and looked again and still don't see anything in your cup, it's probably because your conscious mind is standing in the way of things. The remedy is to relax, focus on your enquiry and then buy another coffee.

Q: I don't believe in omens. Will it still work?
A: Yes. You don't have to believe in electricity or know how it works for it to light up your house.

Q: I have conflicting symbols. What does that mean?
A: Check where the symbols are placed in the cup. This changes the meaning. It may also mean that things are undecided at this time or that things can go either way. Also, you may wish to look for a third symbol. Importantly though, what does your intuition tell you? What feels right?

Q: I spilt my coffee as I turned it over. Will I get an accurate result?
A: Yes.

Q: I drink white coffee. Can I still read my cup?
A: Absolutely! You just will not be reading the same parts of the cup as espresso drinkers. Pay special attention to the any foam or milk marks around your cup. If you take sugar the dregs of the grains should also be read. These are all what will manifest the Oracle symbols.

Q: How often should I consult the Oracle?
A: I am tempted to say as often as you have a coffee; however I know some of you drink LOTS of coffee! Once a day is fine, more than that, unless it's for something important that's cropped up, is probably too much. If you do have related questions though, having one coffee after another in quick succession is also acceptable.

Q: I love the idea of the 28-Day Self Discovery Plan,
but can I do that for longer than 28 days?
A: Yes, it is a wonderful plan to do for yourself, but it can be quite intense. I would recommend trying it for the first 28 days and then if you wish, continuing it over three 28 day cycles (almost three months). From my experience this is a perfect amount of time for profound changes to occur.

Q: I would like to learn more. Do you conduct workshops?
A: Yes I do. Teaching the Coffee Oracle is such a fun and interesting experience for me that I love to share the art. Often the workshops are conducted in cafes so you get to drink great coffee too! It is such an enjoyable experience to do with a friend or two. I am also very interested in teaching people how to read The Coffee Oracle accurately for others and run specific professional courses for those who wish to follow this path.

Please visit my website
www.themodernwitch.com
for the latest schedule of events.
I hope to meet you soon!

ANIMAL GUIDES

Sometimes there are so many animals in coffee cups that you can almost feel like you are on safari searching for them all!

To make things easier, I have created a handy table featuring a wide variety of animals and their key Oracle attributes. These are listed in addition to the ones already featured in the Symbol Dictionary. I hope you find it useful.

ANIMAL	KEY ORACLE MESSAGES
Badger	Finding your way through the dark, joy, trust
Bandicoot	Decision-making, honesty, temperance, moderation
Bear	Being prepared, invulnerability, strength, protection
Beaver	Home building, industriousness, vigilance, peacefulness
Buffalo	Protection, justice, gentle strength
Chameleon	Mastering change, transformation, sexual games, transformation
Cheetah	Speed, acceleration, focus
Cicada	Partnership, joy, blessings
Cockatoo	Intelligence, ingenuity, speaking up
Cougar	Fury, lack of remorse, cunning, hunting and seeking, freedom, power
Crow	Legal matters, justice, trust, messenger
Dingo	Solitude, independence, play, strategy
Dugong	Gentleness, secrets, feminine power, the ocean
Echidna	Innocence, trust, minding your own business

Elk	Stamina, strength, speed, sensual passion
Fox	Stealth, cunning, slyness, sexual attraction, wisdom
Goanna	Wisdom, guidance, speed, agility
Goat	Sacrifice, mischief, fertility
Gorilla	Communication through action, gentle strength
Hare	Fertility, transformation, quick thinking, strength, intuition, traditional witch's animal
Lemur	Dancing, happiness, inquisition
Panda	Surprising strength, solitude, love
Polar Bear	Clarity, intuition, self-trust
Red Panda	Unexpected fierceness, versatility, agility
Reindeer	Masculine power, male potency, stamina
Seal	Playfulness, speed, agility
Seahorse	Balance of the sexes, transformation, protection
Skink	Lust, forward motion, happiness
Skunk	Interconnectedness, dreams, warnings
Snail	Reputation, courage, willpower, self-respect
Snow Leopard	Grace, secrecy, longevity
Sugar Glider	Trust, surrender, leaps of faith, positivity
Tamarin	Preciousness, curiosity, cherishing what you have
Tasmanian Devil	Aggression, stubbornness, honesty, flexibility
Tasmanian Tiger	Rareness, prosperity, integrity, dreams
Wallaby	Nimbleness, flexibility, small leaps forward
Weasel	Ingenuity, discovery, determination, speed
Wombat	Quiet determination, tenacity, persistence, solidness

THE 28 DAY SELF–DISCOVERY PLAN TEMPLATE

Day	Question	Symbol & Interpretation	Actionable Insights
1			
2			
3			
4			
5			
6			
7			
	Week 1 Summary		
8			
9			
10			
11			
12			
13			
14			
	Week 2 Summary		
15			
16			
17			
18			
19			
20			

Day	Question	Symbol & Interpretation	Actionable Insights
21			
	Week 3 Summary		
22			
23			
24			
25			
26			
27			
28			

My Key Findings: _____

_____

_____

_____

My Key Actionable Insights which I promise to act upon immediately:

_____

_____

_____

_____

ACKNOWLEDGEMENTS

The very first metaphysical book I ever read was Louise L Hay's classic, *You Can Heal Your Life*. It made me re-think the way I saw the world and, moreover, think about the things I didn't see. It started me on the path to a bigger, wider world. To be published by Hay House is not only a great joy to me, but in some ways it's a kind of kismet, a circumnavigation of a full circle that I can now hope will expand even more widely and fully.

I thank my Australian publisher, the indomitable Leon Nacson for his belief, guidance and facilitation into the world of Hay House. I would also like to thank the entire team at Hay House Australia who have helped shape and design this book into a work which I am sure will attract many readers.

To my husband Adam, I express my deepest love and gratitude for your complete faith in me and your persistent reminders to allow and receive. No coffee, no matter how good, stimulates and inspires me as much as you do.

To the Goddesses in my kitchen and in the cafés, I am grateful to you all, in particular Phyllis Tsolakis, Angela Heise, Lisa Foster and the godmother, Robin Stein. Thank you all for stirring the pot.

To the Gods in the kitchen and the cafes in particular: David Skapinker and David Garland. Thank you all for keeping things on the boil. Thank you Lee and Stephanie at Sticky and Moo's for letting us take over your café for the photo shoot. Glenn Kelly, great photographs!

Many thanks to Ro Markson and the North Sydney Career Coven members for your support.

And, finally, a debt of gratitude to all the wonderful baristas I have met in the making of this book, in particular Chris and Thom. You are all the priests and priestesses of the coffee craft. You can bring back a smile, warm a heart, radiate energy, offer clarity, or at the very least give a gift of space for all the senses in a takeaway cardboard cup. You are all a bigger part of the spiritual world than you realise!

We hope you enjoyed this Hay House book.
If you'd like to receive a free catalogue featuring
additional Hay House books and products,
or if you'd like information about the
Hay Foundation, please contact:

Hay House Australia Pty. Ltd.,
18/36 Ralph St., Alexandria NSW 2015
Phone: 612-9669-4299 • Fax: 612-9669-4144
www.hayhouse.com.au

Published and distributed in the USA by:
Hay House, Inc.,
P.O. Box 5100, Carlsbad, CA 92018-5100
Phone: (760) 431-7695 • Fax: (760) 431-6948
www.hayhouse.com®

Published and distributed in the United Kingdom by:
Hay House UK, Ltd., 292B Kensal Rd., London W10 5BE
Phone: 44-20-8962-1230 • Fax: 44-20-8962-1239
www.hayhouse.co.uk

*Published and distributed in the
Republic of South Africa by:*
Hay House SA (Pty), Ltd., P.O. Box 990, Witkoppen 2068
Phone/Fax: 27-11-706-6612 • orders@psdprom.co.za

Published in India by: Hay House Publishers India,
Muskaan Complex, Plot No. 3, B-2, Vasant Kunj,
New Delhi 110 070
Phone: 91-11-4176-1620 • Fax: 91-11-4176-1630
www.hayhouse.co.in

Distributed in Canada by: Raincoast,
9050 Shaughnessy St., Vancouver, B.C. V6P 6E5
Phone: (604) 323-7100 • Fax: (604) 323-2600
www.raincoast.com

Tune in to **HayHouseRadio.com**® for the best in
inspirational talk radio featuring top Hay House authors!
And, sign up via the Hay House Australia Website to receive
the Hay House online newsletter and stay informed about what's
going on with your favourite authors. You'll receive
announcements about Discounts and Offers, Special Events,
Product Highlights, Giveaways, and more!
www.hayhouse.com.au